The Living Past

CW00670261

A selection of articles on
Hull and East Yorkshire
previously published in the
Hull Daily Mail

by

John Markham

Highgate of Beverley

Highgate Publications (Beverley) Limited
2001

i

British Library Cataloguing in Publication Data.
A catalogue record for this book is available from the British Library.

ISBN 1 902645 26 X

Published by

Highgate of Beverley

Highgate Publications (Beverley) Limited
4 Newbegin, Beverley, HU17 8EG. Telephone (01482) 886017

Printed by Highgate Print Limited
4 Newbegin, Beverley, HU17 8EG. Telephone (01482) 886017

Foreword

by
John Meehan, Editor of the *Hull Daily Mail*
.

In the spring of 1996 the *Hull Daily Mail* asked John Markham to contribute ten articles on local history. When he handed in his tenth article he enquired, 'What next?' The answer was, 'Carry on idefinitely.' Over five years later his column, **The Living Past,** is still going strong.

In spite of his many books and contributions to academic journals, John considers his articles for the *Mail* are probably the most important historical work he has ever done. He sees no reason why history should not be written in a readable style which makes it more accessible and attractive to more people. The continuing popularity of **The Living Past** speaks for itself.

When he began his series of articles there was no intention of producing a book. But a number of readers have suggested that the time has come to put them into a more permanent form. I am happy to be one of the many who welcome this first selection.

Authors's Preface

These Articles are substantially as they appeared in the *Hull Daily Mail*, though for reasons of space certain passages had to be omitted from the previously published versions. The titles are my own, not necessarily those which appeared in the press. I have added subtitles where the subject is not immediately apparent.

Inevitably over a period repetitions occur. Where this leads to unnecessary duplication I have made omissions; those which remain are, I think, relevant to their context.

I am grateful for the response to this continuing series of articles and, as this selection shows, I am indebted to those readers who have offered additional information.

John Markham

Contents

THE COMMUTER FROM PAULL

Anthony Bannister

When, at long last, the weather becomes warmer and local people feel the need for an easy outing which provides a breath of fresh air, it's then that Paull comes into its own.

Nowadays motorists are directed to a car park outside the village where they can sit and contemplate the water or walk along the Humber bank until their energy runs out. It is a car park with a difference. This pleasant riverside spot was once the site of High Paull House, demolished earlier this century but in the 1850s the home of one of the area's most flamboyant characters, Anthony Bannister, who has a lasting place in local history as the maker of modern Withernsea.

The Humber played a major role in his life. Born in 1817, the son of an employee of Hull Dock Company and apprenticed to a leading shipowner, he established himself as a successful merchant of coal and fish. It was his love of sailing which presumably brought him to Paull, first to Boreas Hill and then, with an ever-increasing family, to the very edge of the river at High Paull, a house which offered a tremendous advantage : he could commute to his office in Hull by water. He was Vice Commodore of the Royal Yorkshire Yacht Club, owned two vessels, the *Royal* and the *Sapphire*, and his delight, said the press, was to go back and forwards between Hull and Paull in a yacht steered by himself.

Heavily bearded Victorian faces tended to give a venerable appearance to men who were still young, and Bannister was only in his 30s when he was at the height of his career. He had been elected to Hull Council in 1845, was sheriff four years later, and twice served as mayor, in 1851-2 and 1855-6. What could be more fitting than the Admiral of the Humber sailing grandly into Hull from his riverside residence at Paull?

Bannister was the archetypal Yorkshireman who prided himself on speaking his mind, a fearless advocate of what he believed to be right, even when he stood alone, roaring at anyone who dared to oppose him, in an accent as broad as his shoulders: 'Deant tell me, Oi woant have it, for Oi knoa better!'

He was also a man of vision, and it was his initiative which led to the opening, in 1854, of the Withernsea railway, a line which he believed would benefit Holderness agriculture at the same time as creating a seaside resort as popular on the East Coast as Brighton on the South. His ambitious plans were not fulfilled, but Withernsea was far from being a failure, for the much-lamented railway took thousands of day trippers for a memorable day at the seaside, and the resort's contribution to human happiness has been immense.

His death, in 1878, though sudden, was not inappropriate. He developed a cold while taking part in a regatta and, claiming that he was 'about all right', spent the last full day of his life at Withernsea. In the evening he returned by train, first to Hull and then to Hessle, where he had moved from Paull, and where he died during the night.

Headstrong and impetuous, he could be an infuriating man who aroused hatred as well as admiration, but even his critics were ready to admit that, after all, 'his heart was in the right place'.

Anthony Bannister.
Martin T. Craven, The Hull to Withernsea Railway 1854-1964 *(1997).*

SAINTS GALORE

St. John Fisher and St. John of Beverley

Local history has a habit of turning up far from home, and there is always a pleasurable glow of recognition when you're miles from East Yorkshire and come across a name or an object which has local links.

In a country house in Berkshire, for example, there's an old walking stick which has particular historical interest for us because it belonged to St. John Fisher, born in Beverley in 1469, the son of a local merchant, Robert Fisher, at No. 58 Flemingate according to tradition.

The house now there, however, dates only from the late 17th century, though it could, of course, have been erected on the site of an older building. On the other hand (history is rarely simple!), his father was buried in St. Mary's Church, possibly an indication that the family lived in the northern part of the town.

Fisher had a distinguished career both as an academic and a churchman. Ordained in 1491, he rose to become Bishop of Rochester, Chancellor of Cambridge University and founder of St. John's College, Cambridge. Unfortunately, he lived in troubled times and, when Henry VIII broke with Rome in 1534, he refused to acknowledge the King as head of the Church in England. He was condemned to death and, already old by Tudor standards, he leant on his ebony walking stick, on 22 June 1535, as he staggered towards the execution block on Tower Hill. It was 400 years before he was declared a saint.

Statue of St. John of Beverley in the Minster.

Some historical items are of doubtful ancestry, but this is a relic which appears to be completely authentic. After Fisher's execution it was rescued by a friar, John Hildesley, handed down in his family and, when Mary Hildesley married, it passed into her husband's family, the Eystons of Hendred House, Berkshire, where it remains. I haven't so far had an opportunity of seeing it, but the present owner, Mr. Thomas Eyston, tells me that he often shows it to visitors.

Beverley has the rare distinction of being able to claim two saints. St. John of Beverley had served as Bishop of Hexham and then Bishop of York before retiring, in the early 8th century, to spend his last years in quiet meditation in his own monastery 'in the wood of the men of Deira', not Beverley by name but, in view of Beverley's wooded terrain and archaeological evidence, sufficient proof for most of us that this was Beverley and John's monastery the religious settlement which developed into the Beverley Minster of today.

John had ordained the historian, Bede, and it was he who described the healing miracles of John which local tradition associates with Bishop Burton, Cherry Burton and, more definitely, Watton Abbey. John's canonisation in 1037 and the many pilgrims his posthumous fame brought to Beverley were an important factor in the growth of the town.

In recent years interest has been focused on the local links of Mary Ward, not officially a saint but the founder of an order of nuns. Most people know about John and Christopher Wright of Welwick, conspirators in the Gunpowder Plot of 1605, but often ignored is their sister, Ursula, who married Marmaduke Ward and became the mother of Mary Ward (1585-1645). As a young girl Mary spent five years in Welwick with her formidable Catholic grandmother, probably crucial years of lasting influence on her in her later hazardous journeys throughout Europe at a time when religious conflicts were intense and cruel.

Happily, we are now able to honour people of character on whichever side of the religious divide their loyalties lay.

INNS – THE 'LOCAL' IN LOCAL HISTORY

In history at least, inns and churches have very close links. The village pub often stands near the parish church, a lingering visual reminder of the moral obligation to offer hospitality to travellers. Names such as Cross Keys (the Papal symbol) are now the barely noticed reminders of the Church's traditional role in providing sustenance for body as well as soul.

Even in a more secular age this tradition of hospitality lives on. An inn is still a 'house' (though 'public' because it's open to all, unlike the private one where you need an invitation), the landlord is 'mine host' and the people he entertains are guests, not customers.

The late Miss Grace Morley, whose family owned the Beverley Arms through three generations from 1852 to 1920, told me that the Morleys regarded it as their home. There was no obvious distinction between public and private quarters, and those who came were treated, and expected to behave, as guests.

Looking back, she was amused at the carefree way valuable silver was left on unguarded display. A press report of October 1815 shows that it *was* a risk. William Jackson pleaded guilty at the Quarter Sessions to stealing ten silver teaspoons from the Beverley Arms and, in spite of several witnesses to his previous good behaviour, received six months' imprisonment, a lenient sentence for that period.

Inns feature prominently in local history because they were the venue for so many social and public events. Before village and parish halls existed, they provided accommodation for such varied purposes as election headquarters, meetings of the clergy, courts of law and inquests. Frequently they are mentioned in newspaper reports of local organisations. In February 1905 one such account described proceedings at the annual meeting of the historic friendly society, the Death Brief at the Dacre Arms, Brandesburton: 'About 60 members turned up to supper, and the rest of the evening was spent in a convivial manner. Several songs were sung by members of the Brief.'

Catering for the needs of travellers made adequate stabling essential, especially so in market towns, and at their peak the Cross Keys, Beverley, had stables for 50 horses, the old Tiger in North Bar Within for 46, and the Beverley Arms for 40. Inn signs throughout East Yorkshire pay tribute to the importance of the horse in agriculture, transport and sport.

The former Tiger Inn.
(Gary Sargeant)

The Black Horse (Atwick and Roos), the White Horse (Easington and Ottringham), and the Nag's Head (Burstwick, Preston and Routh) have some of the most popular names, but more unusual are the Altisidora (Bishop Burton), the Nancy (Burton Pidsea) and the Rockingham (Lockington), all commemorating prize-winning race horses.

Many pub names are long established, but a sizeable number have undergone change, sometimes occasioned by national events. Lund has its Wellington, Beverley its Lord Nelson, and both Kirkburn and Hedon have a Queens Head named on the accession of Victoria in 1837. Name changing is certainly one tradition which is alive and kicking.

THE BEVERLEY PRISON WHICH WAS NO HOLIDAY CAMP
East Riding House of Correction, Norfolk Street

For tourists – and local historians – prisons don't have quite the appeal of stately homes and medieval churches.

But one local prison, the East Riding House of Correction in Beverley, has more interest than most penal institutions, not least because of the existence of a vivid description of its harsh regime written by Robert Peddie, an unusually literate prisoner.

In some ways it was remarkable that the prison was built where it was, off New Walk, a rural lane until it was developed in the late 18th century as a fashionable promenade where those who belonged to the town's élite could take elegant exercise and display themselves in all their finery to the admiring or envious eyes of their equals. An imposing Sessions House had been built there in 1807, not only as a court of law but also as a venue for the formalities of parliamentary elections and other public events. Then, three years later, the prison complex was developed at its rear, convenient no doubt for the quick despatch of convicted defendants but hardly in keeping with the genteel character the area was acquiring.

Anyone who served a sentence there would have no desire to repeat the experience. As its name made clear, you went there to have your misconduct corrected by an unappetising diet of plain food combined with hard work and moral training and, so the theory went, leave determined to offend no more.

The days were packed with long hours of work, for

Central building – formerly the Turnkey's house.

prisoners had to earn their keep. Weaving, making lights from rushes, and 'dressing' flax were all tolerable, if tedious occupations. More arduous was breaking stones, but nowhere near as unpleasant as working on the treadmill which crushed chalk into whiting.

It was the cruelty of the treadmill which stirred the indignation of Robert Peddie, who had been convicted along with four fellow Chartists, members of a Radical reform movement, of involvement in an outbreak of public disorder in Bradford and sentenced to three years' hard labour.

Peddie's belief that he was a political prisoner, unjustly convicted, added to his grievances. To him the prison was the 'hell hole' of Beverley and its most hated feature the treadmill, a perpetually moving staircase, which he had to tread for what amounted to a daily total of 1,000 steps in a direct perpendicular line. The sweat pouring from his body and the dizziness which overtook him well before he had completed his stint made it torture enough without one further humiliation: the treadmill was open at one side and spectators could watch the prisoners 'caged like beasts in a menagerie'.

The fear that inmates would be brutalised by contact with more hardened criminals was counteracted by the introduction of the Silent System of total isolation which aimed to prohibit any prisoner from speaking to another. There was certainly cause for concern about young offenders. The 1841 Census revealed that one prisoner was as young as 13 – Joseph Spivey, a shoemaker's apprentice – and there were more than a dozen only a year or two older.

Yet, even in the bleakest conditions kindness can lighten the gloom. In 1828 the local press reported that one former prisoner had left sixpence to the 'dear little friendless boy' who gave him 'what skilly he could and sometimes pieces of bread'.

The prison was closed in 1878 and, surprisingly, its buildings converted into smart houses in what is now Norfolk Street. Evidence of the former prison can still be identified but, fortunately, nothing remains of its forbidding atmosphere.

STREET NAMES – A WAY INTO THE PAST

One of the most intriguing routes into the past is through street names, often a link with the early beginnings of a town or village and with the people who later lived there.

A word of warning, though! Street names can be dangerously misleading. Over the centuries pronunciation and spelling may have changed out of all recognition, and what seems an obvious explanation isn't necessarily correct.

The oldest names were not officially agreed, as they are today, by a committee, but developed naturally as the most practical way of describing a street, either by its location or its business activities. Northside (Patrington) means what it says, and Hornsea is just one of many places which have key thoroughfares – such as Westgate – named after the points of the compass.

'Gate' in an old name is a version of the Old Norse word, *gata*, meaning 'street', and does not in itself indicate the existence of a town gate in that vicinity. The 'High' in Highgate (Beverley) or High Street (Patrington) means 'principal' or 'main', and Hedon people often refer to St. Augustine's Gate by the simpler title, 'Main Street', a name which is common in American towns.

Names such as Newbegin (Beverley) and Hornsea) have their origin in obsolete words which once made immediate sense: 'niwe biggin' meant simply 'new building' and described an area where such developments were taking place. Finkle Street, which occurs all over the East Riding, comes from a northern dialect word, 'fenkl', meaning 'corner' or 'elbow', and Finkle Streets usually incorporate a bend, or lead to one, though, rather confusingly, not the one in Bishop Burton.

Railway Street may no longer carry a note of romance but it is proof of the importance attached in the 19th century to this magnificent new form of transport and the pride people took in having their own station. It is very fitting that Withernsea should have a Bannister Street in honour of the man who transformed its character by making it the terminal point of a railway. High Brighton Street is a poignant reminder of his ambition to create a seaside resort on the East Coast at least as successful as the one on the South. Withernsea has loyally commemorated a number of important men, but, with the passing of time, the people who actually inspired Cheverton Avenue and Young, George and Cammidge Streets tend to be overlooked.

Blucher Lane, Beverley, seems at first sight a mystery. Would Beverlonians really have felt an urge to name a street after Gebhard von Blucher, a Prussian soldier, who admittedly proved a vital ally of Wellington at the Battle of Waterloo? Indirectly, in fact, this probably happened. The well-known historian and journalist, Paul Johnson, has stated that 'Blucher' became the most popular name for dogs (presumably of the more ferocious type) after Waterloo, and an old Beverley resident recalled that a family named Catterson, who lived in the lane in the 1820s, kept a huge dog named Blucher chained up in their yard. No doubt those who ventured fearfully past regarded this particular byway, dominated by the intimidating animal, as Blucher's or Blucher Lane.

Sometimes the most unlikely explanation turns out to be correct.

THE SYKES – AN EAST RIDING FAMILY

Sledmere is the place which automatically comes to mind when you mention the name, Sykes, but this important local family spread its influence over the whole East Riding.

Roos in Holderness plays a significant part in their story, for the Rev. Mark Sykes, who was Rector there for 48 years, became head of the family after the death of his elder brother, Richard, in 1761.

Mark's son, the multi-talented Christopher, was more prominent both locally and nationally. As well as being co-founder of the East Riding Bank, he had a major impact on the Yorkshire Wolds through a massive programme of enclosures and the planting of trees and hedges. As his own architect, he re-designed Sledmere House, and he was M.P. for Beverley 1784-90.

When he was offered a baronetcy he showed great filial devotion by asking for it first to be given to his father, and so, from 28 March 1783, we have the grandly named Rev. Sir Mark Sykes. He enjoyed the honour for only a short time, and, after his death on 14 September that year, Christopher duly inherited the title.

Although one would expect Mark, the Rector, to be buried at Roos, I was surprised to discover that a memorial in the church records that 'the mortal remains of Christopher', who died in Bristol in 1801, also rest there in the family vault.

This was not the end of the Roos connection. Another Christopher, brother of the great Wolds character, Sir Tatton, the 4th baronet, was Rector of Roos and also Hilston. By now the Sykes were substantial land owners in Holderness; the Rev. Christopher was a leading member of the local farming community and by all accounts a well-respected man. He died aged 83 in 1857 and was also buried at Roos.

The Sykes link with Beverley was strengthened in 1830 when Daniel Sykes of Raywell, a descendant of a junior branch of the family, was elected one of the town's two M.P.s.

Born in 1766 and a barrister by profession, he was a a man of cultivated tastes who would have preferred to

Daniel Sykes.

spend his life enjoying the works of literature in the library of his pleasantly situated house. But duty called. Daniel had a strong sense of public service and believed firmly in the need for reform. He opposed slavery, supported press freedom, wanted more men to have the vote, believed in education for all and disliked religious intolerance.

When Hull lacked a Whig candidate in 1820 he overcame his reluctance to surrender his private and scholarly life and entered the fray, though, after ten years, his Hull supporters were muttering that his views were too advanced for their liking, and he transferred to Beverley. In a hard-fought contest he won the second seat, but wisely asked to be excused the ordeal of the ceremony in which victorious candidates were carried aloft in a ceremonial chair round the Market Cross, exposed to the cheer of supporters and the insults and missiles of opponents. Unfortunately Parliament was dissolved after only a year, and at the 1831 election Daniel was too ill to stand. He died in 1832.

This Beverley-Sykes link was revived when yet another Christopher was M.P. 1865-8, later representing the East Riding and Buckrose, and Sir Mark Sykes was M.P. for Hull 1911-19.

All evidence which proves that there is more to the Sykes than Sledmere.

WHAT THE PAPERS SAID

History from local newspapers

Nothing brings back the flavour of the past so immediately and powerfully as an old newspaper.

History books describe the great events, painstakingly recorded and analysed by experts who have had time to consider them from every viewpoint and to form a balanced judgement. But in those closely printed columns of old newspapers you find a vivid picture of everyday life, the trivial as well as the important, in all its muddled variety.

What political tome could be as fresh as this press report of a meeting in Beckside, Beverley, in 1906, when interest was so great that a great number of disappointed people were unable to hear a speech by Stanley Wilson, Tory candidate for Holderness in the general election of that year? They missed what the paper described as 'pantomime politics' when one elector, James Bugg, a shoemaker, asked for a private session with Wilson on the subject of taxation: 'Now,

From the Hull Daily Mail, *10 December 1936*

just one minute of you. I should like to have a bit of higher education on this fiscal education and hand-sewn shoemaking, and, if you will come one day to my place and be measured for a pair we could have a quiet talk on the matter.'

Not surprisingly, the report continued, 'The meeting gave itself up to hearty laughter', and there were more laughs when Wilson's confident claim that he would be elected was greeted with shouts of, 'You won't be!' from Liberals in the audience.

A striking feature of the 'small ads' well into this century was the number of jobs on offer and sought in domestic service. One typical edition of the *Hull Daily Mail* contained 57 such advertisements, and there were no niceties about 'mother's help' or 'cleaning lady'. Social attitudes of the time were revealed in the directness of the language so unselfconsciously used. 'Wanted strong girl' or 'woman' left no one in any doubt about the arduousness of the work. Applicants had to be 'respectable', a 'character' was often required, and some employers who did not want their domestics contaminated by city ways added, 'Country girl preferred'. It was not uncommon to show quite blatant religious discrimination and include such phrases as 'Churchwoman preferred'.

Just as domestic service provided a major job market for female labour, so did agriculture for males. Holderness clay was not for the faint-hearted or feeble-handed, and an advertisement in 1910 offered a challenging opportunity: 'Wanted a good strong plough lad. Must be used to strong land. Apply R. Mook, Keyingham'. Less physically demanding was a vacancy in the vicarage at North Frodingham: 'Wanted a youth to live indoors, about 14 years old, to look after a small pony and make himself useful in the home'.

It was not all work. Because holidays were shorter and less frequent than today, they probably provided more intense pleasure, and excellent train services made it possible to use that precious free day for a trip to the coast. On August Bank Holiday 1911, the press reported that 20 trains had left Hull for Hornsea and 18 for Withernsea where 'Each train brought in its load of pleasure seekers who made the most of the holiday. The various entertainments were capitally patronised and, though there was plenty of life in the town, it is satisfactory to note that the crowds were orderly and quiet.'

No shortage of public transport and no lager louts. Happy Days!

AS OTHERS SEE US

Celia Fiennes, James Boswell, Mary Wollstonecraft and George Head

Seeing ourselves as others see us is supposed to be a useful exercise – though another person's opinion may be no more accurate than our own. But the impressions of familiar local places seen in the past by travellers and visitors are always intriguing, and sometimes the only source of information available.

One of the most attractive accounts is by an adventurous lady, Celia Fiennes, who toured the north of England on horseback in 1697. From York she rode to Beverley, a very fine town in her opinion, with good streets, buildings that were 'new and pretty lofty', and so many public wells that she was reminded of Holland. She was fascinated by the memorials and tombs in the Minster and so impressed by St. Mary's ('very large and good') that, like many tourists, when she first entered the town she mistook it for the Minster.

Nearly a century later, on 22 May 1778, the diarist, James Boswell, arrived in Beverley and put up for the night at the Tiger in North Bar Within. Everything there pleased him, and, in spite of a hangover caused by supping 'very heartily', he was still sufficiently enthusiastic to be up at seven the next morning and sightseeing before breakfast. Beverley he summed up as a 'pretty idle town', his own way, I suppose, of indicating that it was an elegant place of residence for people of means, and, as far as he could see, without much industry.

Less complimentary about the charms of Georgian Beverley was Mary Wollstonecraft, the radical writer and pioneering feminist, who became the mother-in-law of the poet, Shelley. She spent an unhappy childhood there in a family permanently short of cash and with a father who was often drunk and violent. When, in 1795, she made a quick return visit, after a tempestuous career which included a period in France during the Revolution, she found that the town of 20 years before seemed to have shrunk, 'and, when I found that many of the inhabitants had lived in the same houses ever since I left it, I could not help wondering how they could thus have vegetated, whilst I was running over a world of sorrow, snatching at pleasure and throwing off prejudices'.

For Holderness there is an atmospheric account of a journey made by Sir George Head in 1835. On his way from Hull to Patrington by coach he counted 25

Hildyard Arms, Patrington

windmills before he had travelled a mile, but, as he moved further out into the country, he was 'disappointed with the condition of the land; for, instead of seeing the high state of agriculture I had anticipated, I found fields overrun with coarse tore grass, in many parts blotchy and covered with thistles'. There were none of the 'stately Holderness cows' that he expected: 'I never saw a handsome beast all the time I was here.' He was, though, impressed by the size of the arable fields, fenced by 'lofty, solid, impenetrable quick hedges', and by farms with fine outbuildings, 'a handsome cluster of stacks and surrounded by a belt of thriving plantations, the whole together, seen from a distance, like a little village'.

In Patrington the Hildyard Arms was doing a roaring trade. Farmers in hob-nailed boots clumped up and down stairs with a sample bag of corn in one hand and a glass of gin in the other, doing business with corn dealers upstairs who shipped Holderness corn from Patrington Haven to the highly populated West Riding.

Motorists familiar with Hedon Road may look back longingly to the peaceful scene described by a *Hull Daily Mail* writer in 1929: 'There were no pedestrians on the broad footpath, and hardly any traffic on the road; a few motor buses were on their way to Hull, and now and then a little motor car would slip quietly by in the opposite direction, and a jogging horse-drawn market cart or two, but otherwise the moon and I had the world to ourselves for most of the way.'

Not many years later, in 1933, J. B. Priestley visited East Yorkshire when he was working on his very readable book, *English Journey*. When he reached Bishop Burton he felt that this was a place where he could settle and become 'a bookish hermit', and, like so many more, he was amazed by his first sight of the Minster in all its magnificence.

It was a corner of England which appealed to him, a long way from anywhere but where you felt that it was a good thing to be a long way from anywhere – an opinion which many will share.

BURTON CONSTABLE HALL

Burton Constable Hall has a special place in my affections. It was the first stately home I ever visited, on a privileged occasion when it was still a very private residence.

Hundreds of country houses are now open to the public and it's no longer a novelty to stroll nonchalantly into a vast entrance hall and through grand saloons filled with valuable antiques, but nothing can equal the amazement of that first experience. Even so, there is still a thrill and a surprise when this impressive and sophisticated building appears, always unexpectedly, in the depths of the Holderness countryside. On a winter evening when the Hall is being used for a function, floodlights focused on its magnificent east front transform it into something even more romantic and it looks as unreal and insubstantial as the backcloth to a play.

Though it may seem a perfect architectural composition, designed to be exactly as it is today, its appearance, like that of most great houses, has changed drastically over the centuries.

The Constable family of the Middle Ages lived at Halsham and it was only in the 16th century that Sir John Constable acquired property at what then was called simply Burton, moved to the present site, and by rebuilding and enlarging the medieval tower house that stood there erected much of what remains today. Then in the 18th century William Constable carried out major alterations, in particular adding another storey and increasing its grandeur. He was also the man to whom the present interior owes so much. Fortunately for later generations, he was a man of taste as well as wealth. Steeped in the traditions of classical design, he employed craftsmen of both national and local reputation to create an artistic masterpiece as the appropriate setting for a cultured man of means.

The Great Hall, the first room seen by visitors, is the grandest of introductions to what is to follow: the dignified Dining Room, the Hall with its cantilevered

staircase on which guests at hunt balls sat in all their finery, the Blue Drawing Room where in the early 19th century Sir Thomas Aston Clifford Constable took his elegant breakfast, gazing through French windows at a statue of a stag in the far distance, and so on to the Ballroom and up to the Long Gallery where gentle exercise could be taken in comfort when the weather outside was too inclement for walking in the gardens and the park.

Anyone who has not been to Burton Constable for some time will be surprised by the number of additional rooms now open , including some furnished colourfully and ornately by Sir Thomas's first wife, Lady Marianne, who had a particular liking for French design and decor.

Maintaining any house can be expensive and for a house of this size it can be prohibitive. In 1992 Burton Constable Hall came under the control of the Burton Constable Foundation and the house now looks far brighter and better than many will remember it.

One small room of great significance in the family story is the chapel. Being Roman Catholic, the Constables were barred from taking up what would have been their normal position in public life, a form of discrimination which did at least give William Constable the freedom to devote his time and money to intellectual and artistic matters and to beautifying his home.

Apart from the Hall itself, two other buildings with Constable connections are worth a mention. One is the Catholic Church at Marton, built in 1789 under the patronage of William Constable, deliberately situated in a secluded spot and with the appearance of a Georgian manor house so that it did not draw unnecessary attention to itself at a time when religious differences were intense.

The other building is a Holderness landmark. The attractive if melancholy mausoleum at the ancestral village, Halsham, completed in 1802 and holding the remains of the early Constables who had originally been buried in the parish church.

Burton Constable Hall.

The opening of country houses to the public has given them a new role as social and cultural centres. Burton Constable Hall is now the venue for many functions and concerts and the Friends of Burton Constable is an organisation arranging its own programme. One last thought. After the last war there was a proposal to create a massive overspill development at Burton Constable to house those who could not be accommodated within the existing boundaries of Hull. If the plan had been implemented we should now be discussing a massive estate at Burton Constable rather than Bransholme.

A CHURCH WITH A LOO
St. Margaret's Church, Hilston

Hilston Church, dedicated, most unusually, to St. Margaret of Scotland, has been very much in my thoughts recently as I've taken part in two days of lectures and visits focused on the life and work of the man who designed it: the eminent Bridlington-born architect, Francis Johnson, who died in 1995.

It stands, very noticeably but in no way ostentatiously, in a pleasant part of Holderness which has a particular appeal for me, and its nearness to the coast has been a major factor in its history.

A dignified Victorian church occupied the site until 18 August 1941, when a German plane which had been involved in the blitz on Hull demolished it with a final bomb before making its escape over the North Sea. But the religious associations of this piece of ground are centuries-old.

St. Margaret's Church, Hilston.

There was a small Norman church here, built of local cobbles and still in use after the mid-19th century, though by then it was in an appalling state of disrepair, damp inside and its outer walls overrun with ivy.

Fortunately for Hilston, the Rector at this critical time was the Reverend Christopher Sykes, younger brother of the fourth baronet, Sir Tatton, and it was through the patronage of Sir Tatton and Lady Sykes that money was provided to engage J. L. Pearson, an architect of national repute, to replace the decayed church with something more fitting for their relation and more pleasing to Victorian taste.

In 1861 the Rector's namesake nephew, another Christopher, laid the foundation stone of the new church, and a year later it was consecrated, a much more sophisticated building than the one it replaced, beautified with Purbeck marble, Minton tiles and an alabaster pulpit and font. Interestingly, however, continuity was maintained by re-erecting the Norman doorway from its predecessor.

Then came the disaster of the Second World War, and the people of Hilston had to use a house for their services as a temporary expedient, which in the event lasted far longer than anyone anticipated. This was the only time I saw the Victorian church, in its ruined state, when, for years after the War, it seemed that it had gone for ever.

Yet the wheels of bureaucracy were slowly moving behind the scenes and, after considerable negotiation, a payment was received from the government department set up to compensate those who had suffered through war damage, though on condition that the money was used for a new church on the same site as the old.

Francis Johnson was appointed architect and Canon Graham Christie, who was then Rector, has told me how he gave him his brief. He wanted a church which was not too large for a small congregation ('In a few hundred years it will go over the cliff!' he warned), and Johnson came up with the idea of a gallery which did not normally require heating but which doubled the seating capacity to 100 on such special occasions as weddings. The Rector also wanted a church with a loo and a wash-basin: he had a busy round of parishes on a Sunday and there were times when he needed to clean up after changing a wheel between churches.

His ideas for the east window were equally clear. Everything it featured was to be associated with the life of St. Margaret, and the predominant blue and white represented the sea lapping the flowers on the Holderness coast. There was symbolism too in the rounded altar steps, like the waves of the sea, and in the marguerites in the altar rail.

Not everything was lost in 1941. A local farmer, Mr. A. R. H. Furley, had stored pieces of stained glass and other items which had been rescued; the glass was now skilfully incorporated into a window on the north side of the church, with memorials that survived unscathed placed on the wall nearby. The crowning touch was the re-use of the Norman doorway, already once re-cycled, and now triumphantly restored as proof of the strength of a tradition which has defied the battering of life's disasters. In 1956 the foundation stone of the third St. Margaret's Church was formally laid, and the building was consecrated by the Archbishop of York in 1957.

It is, I think, a minor masterpiece, one of the best buildings Francis Johnson designed and one of the most successful of post-war churches. Scandinavian in style and quite different in appearance from the local churches with which we are all familiar, it nevertheless fits perfectly into the landscape of an area which has strong historic links with the countries of Northern Europe. Inside, it impresses by its tranquillity, its lightness, and the air of effortless perfection which is the hallmark of a Francis Johnson building.

This simplicity, of course, is all an illusion and can only be achieved by endless attention to every detail. For most readers, too, a visit to Hilston Church involves a fairly long journey, but it's one which is well worth making.

WEEKEND DISORDER IN BEVERLEY IS NO NEW THING

The last use of the stocks

Local libraries contain excellent collections of material on local history, but I had to visit the British Library outpost in north London to see copies of the late-19th-century newspaper, the *Hull Express*, which was not available nearer to home.

At first sight it looked an unappetising read, with acres of small dark print unrelieved by pictures, but any suggestion of boredom was dispelled by its fascinating contents. Particularly interesting was a series of reminiscences written anonymously by 'An Old Freeman of Beverley', still alive in 1883 and able to look back over most of the 19th century.

One event he recalled with undimmed memory was the last occasion anyone was placed in the stocks at Beverley. He was only a boy at the time and hurrying home from school one Monday morning when he noticed a crowd gathered round the Market Cross. Pushing his way through, he soon realised what all the fuss was about. There in the stocks under the Cross was a man he recognised, Jim Brigham, dirty and unwashed and altogether 'a very sorry spectacle', who, earlier that day, had been brought before the Mayor and ordered to be placed there from twelve until two.

His offence, drinking on a Sunday 'during the hours of Divine Service', was hardly unique in Beverley and there was a general feeling that he was the scapegoat for others equally guilty but impossible to arrest without causing more trouble than the act warranted.

It was the custom on a Sunday for the churchwardens to visit all the public houses in their parish and check that only bona fide travellers were drinking while religious services were in progress. No one, however, took this ritual seriously. The expected time of the churchwardens' visit was easy to calculate, and an inn's front door would be locked so that, when the law-enforcement officials arrived, there was adequate time for illicit drinkers to escape through the rear and for the landlord to remove all incriminating evidence.

What made the Sunday morning routine even more of a farce was the positive help the churchwardens gave the lawbreakers. Until elected to their high office, they were often found among the Sabbath drinkers, and consequently came to a mutually beneficial arrangement which gave landlords immunity from arrest and allowed themselves the freedom to resume their old habits once their period as church officials was over.

Unfortunately, their tolerant approach encouraged more to flout the regulations and, as the Old Freeman explained so delicately, 'caused several inveterate topers to indulge their love of drink to such an excess that they actually became a nuisance to the peaceable inhabitants on a Sunday morning by their riotous conduct in the street, often culminating in a fight and causing a crowd to assemble'.

Something, the law-abiders agreed, had to be done. But making an arrest wasn't an easy task for churchwardens, who were often related to the worst offenders and could suffer obvious repercussions in a small community where, in any dispute, family loyalty was supreme.

This was where Jim Brigham had his uses. He was not very bright and had lost the only job he ever held, in racing stables at Malton, through drink. After roaming around the country, he returned to his home town, Beverley, though his only living relation was his sister, a 'fallen woman', with a worse reputation than himself. But, here, the authorities decided, was the sacrificial victim they sought, and one Sunday morning he was taken into custody as he staggered along the street and kept in prison until his appearance before the Mayor the following day. A couple of hours in the stocks was a painful ordeal as well as a humiliation.

Jim was 'seated on a bench that slanted backwards and was lower than the holes in which his legs were placed, thus causing a severe strain on the muscles of the loins and thighs – slight at first, but which, as time passed, became an intense agony of torture'.

There was great sympathy for the victim, but nevertheless his punishment appears to have acted as a deterrent to other potential lawbreakers. He, alas, continued to drink his way along a downhill path between workhouse and prison, and harsh treatment in both those institutions accelerated his decline. At Christmas time one stormy winter he was found dead in a stable behind the King's Head.

The now redundant stocks outlived their last occupant and can still be seen in the Priests' Room at St. Mary's Church.

BEVERLEY v THE REST

The annual football match, c.1820

Football, some television viewers will perhaps agree, is not everyone's idea of the perfect pastime, and there were certainly Beverley residents hostile to the matches played – or, rather, fought – on 'Race Sundays' in the early years of the 19th century.

These were the Sundays preceding the spring and summer race meetings when, according to the 'Old Freeman' whose reminiscences I mentioned last week, a 'tea meeting' was held in the grandstand by 'the tradesmen and better class of inhabitants'. It was all very respectable and quite unlike the contest they surveyed from a sensible distance: a football match between the young men of Beverley and those from the villages around. A goal was scored when one side managed to get the ball to a spot in North Bar Within opposite St. Mary's Church, and the Beverlonians were the usual favourites.

One Sunday in the 1820s the Beverley players were hard pressed and saved only by the remarkable feat of Bob Spence, a butcher, who kicked the ball from the Rose and Crown right over the North Bar. Unfortunately, it raised excitement to such a pitch that crowds rushed

Beverley North Bar and North Bar Without.

through the Bar and collided with the Mayor and his escorting officers who had been attending a service in St. Mary's. Enough was enough, and it was widely known that steps were being taken to prevent a similar occurrence when the next Race Sunday came around.

When it did, it was a perfect April day. Those who opposed any attempt to curb their fun hissed the Mayor as he left church, and at three o'clock the game began. Beverley got control and the pack moved towards the town. At this point, though, a plain-clothed George Ruddock, the bellman, who had been lying in wait on the grass, sprang to his feet, seized the ball and attempted to take it with him over a hedge to his horse which was held by another constable.

The best-laid plans have a habit of going awry. George found the hedge a little too high even to clamber over, he was caught by Bob Pratt, 'a daring pugilist', and dragged mercilessly along its top until he was almost torn to pieces by strong and prickly thorns. Before his capture, however, George had thrown the ball to ' Robert' Kemp, one of the town's sergeants. As he ran to catch it, he slipped, and one of the players hurled a large piece of chalk stone at his head and prevented him from continuing with his official duties. Beverley recaptured the ball and, once again, brought it safely into goal.

But winning the battle is not the same as winning the war. When the next 'Race Sunday' occurred it was summer. More spectators than ever turned out, for there was a strong suspicion that something unusual was about to happen. At first the ball was carried in the direction of Walkington but inevitably the brave Beverlonians regained control. Suddenly there was a cry: 'Look out! The soldiers are coming!' No less a personage than the Mayor, mounted on a grey horse, was riding at the head of a 40-strong troop of militia.

When he read the Riot Act his voice was drowned by the noise of 'offensive allusions to his private life' yelled at him. But the game was up. The soldiers fixed bayonets and advanced, and the players had no option but to accept defeat.

Reminiscences, of course, stand or fall by their accuracy and at this distance of time it is impossible to verify every detail. Directories show that the sergeant was probably William, not Robert, Kemp, but there was a butcher named Robert Spence, and the account does have the ring of truth. In his *History and Antiquities of Beverley (1829)* George Oliver described in more general terms the events leading up to the suppression of the game in 1825. John Williams, Mayor 1824-5, was determined to take action against 'loose young men' profaning the Sabbath. In the struggle some of the constables were 'severely handled', but the culprits were charged with assault and sentenced to hard labour. Writing only four years later, Oliver concluded that 'the practice has been altogether abandoned'.

BACKSTAIRS AT BURTON CONSTABLE

Burton Constable Hall in its heyday needed an army of servants in the rear quarters to service those who occupied the grand apartments at the front, and my recent article on Burton Constable led to a meeting with a lady who worked there 67 years ago and had her own – very vivid – memories of life in a stately home. At her own request, however, I am not disclosing her name.

Now in her 84th year (and looking far younger) she clearly recalls the day in 1929 when, at the age of 16, she went for an interview at Burton Constable, taking the bus to Sproatley and being met by the groom with a pony and trap. She arrived by a back entrance to face a rigorous interview conducted by a formidable housekeeper, who explained her duties and the code of conduct which all staff had to follow: under no circumstances to repeat any of her employers' private conversation she happened to overhear.

Undaunted, she took the job at a salary of 17s. 6d. per calendar month, starting work at 6 am and rarely finishing until after the family had dined. Free time was half a day each week and every other Sunday afternoon, staff were addressed by their surnames, and correct uniform was essential: navy blue dress, whole apron and full cap for mornings, and black dress, small apron and 'Nippy' cap for afternoons.

Her position in the hierarchy was fourth housemaid out of five, and other staff kept were the butler, housekeeper, cook, kitchen maid, scullery maid, groom, footman, and odd job man, as well as gardener and dairy staff. Food was poor, and the very first meal made a

A room providing elegance to residents, work to servants.

strong impression. She was mystified by the number of small pots on the table until the footman explained that twice a week each person was allocated a ration of sugar and butter. For Sunday breakfast there was always one sausage, and even the butler realised that this sparse diet was 'no good for growing girls' and kept back part of the family's richer menu for the younger servants.

Apart from this indirect link, a housemaid's life was worlds apart from that of the family, whom she rarely saw. Staff were allowed to walk in the well-kept grounds on strict instructions never to be seen on the front drive. Occasionally, however, they encountered Lt. Colonel Chichester Constable, whose favourite question was, 'And who are you?' A regime dominated by a very strict housekeeper and a bad-tempered cook did not make for a pleasant atmosphere and staff turnover was high.

A spiral staircase led to a top storey where female staff had their rooms austerely furnished with lumpy flock mattresses and with windows so high that it was necessary for her to stand on a chair to see the meet of the Holderness Hounds at the front. The only amenity was a communal cold tap and it was a hazardous job carrying hot water up the spiral stairs for a hip bath.

Lights out was at 10 p.m. but the girls tried to get upstairs before then and have a fashion parade, dressing in the costumes which had been used in the private theatre and were stored in one of the empty rooms. On one memorable occasion a girl dressed in a white sheet descended the stairs to terrify the unpopular cook who had caused the kitchenmaid to burn her hand badly. The screams were a joy to hear.

After two years the fourth housemaid felt she was experienced enough to take up a better-paid post and worked, first at Rolston Hall, later at Willow Garth, and eventually for the Hudsons in Swanland.

In spite of the hardships, she has no regrets. She met a variety of people, broadened her outlook and took pride in her upward progress. Return journeys, in recent years, to Burton Constable have naturally been full of interest, though it is a shock to see 'all and sundry' walking on that sacred front drive.

TO BE A FARMER'S BOY

Harry Plaxton

Saturday Market Place, Beverley, was buzzing with activity on 23 November, 1927 and the pubs were doing a roaring trade. The Martinmas hirings were in progress, the time of the year when farm servants had an opportunity to find a better 'place' than the one they had known for the past year, and 60 or 70 men and youths were wandering about, hoping for something good to turn up.

Among them was 15-year-old Harry Plaxton who was there with his father. Since leaving school he had already had brief experience on a market garden at Thearne and a smallholding at Ellerker, but this was the real thing: leaving home for a whole year.

His father happened to see an old foreman friend and this led to an introduction to John Elvidge, farmer of Risby Park. The interview that followed was brief and to the point. 'You're not real big,' said Mr. Elvidge, 'but I'll tell you what I'll do – I'll give you 11 "pun" for a year, all in. Here you is – half-a-crown "fest!"' Once the 'fest' [fastener] was accepted, Harry would have been in breach of contract if he had failed to appear.

And so, a week later, he alighted from the bus at Little Weighton and, awkwardly carrying the tin box holding his possessions, started the long walk down Risby Lane. It was nearly six o'clock when he arrived and the welcome was even more abrupt than the interview. He had missed tea and there was no such meal as supper. 'Tha's late!' he was told. 'You can get your old clothes on and get into stables!'

Thereafter, for a year, it was up at 4.30, with clothes and boots 'chucked' downstairs if he failed to respond immediately to his early morning call. The room he shared with two other lads was rather basic, with a corn sack for a carpet, and washing was outside in a tin bowl near the water tub.

As 'Thoddy's Lad' [helping the Third Man], Harry Plaxton had a lowly position in the farm hierarchy and,

when he had finished work in a field, there was no question of leaving. A strict order of precedence was imposed and each man waited to follow his senior in rank.

Horses, too, had priority over humans and, once up, it was out to the stables before being called in to breakfast. The foreman served the men with slices of cold meat, followed by pie and accompanied by a mug of tea, but never could a new pie be cut until the old one was finished.

After a year he took a job with better pay, £18 a year, at Low Baswick near Leven, on a farm managed by foreman George Dawson for Captain Adrian Bethell. Mr. Plaxton, now 84, remembers Mr. Dawson as 'a smashing fellow' and Captain Bethell as 'a perfect gentlemen' who would appear in a chauffeur-driven Sunbeam or on his hunter and have a meal with his employees.

Enormous pride was taken in the horses and Harry became expert at plaiting manes with ribbon and trimming and bobbing tails. There was great pride also in what he describes as 'getting things right', ploughing a straight furrow and drilling in perfect line. Farm-workers in the Leven area would gather at the village fish shop and there was intense rivalry over their skills. Sometimes they would survey each other's fields and hand out insults: 'By God tha's made a right mess of this!' was the nearest to a compliment you could expect.

Now 'Thoddy' and no longer 'lad', Harry next moved to Linley Hill for £26 p.a., and, promoted to Waggoner, transferred to Heigholme Hall, which he still lovingly recalls as 'a wonderful food shop' with the best meals he ever enjoyed. After that came Catfoss Grange.

In the mid-1930s he left farm service for employment with Hull Co-operative Society. It was the end of an important chapter in his life but not a complete break. The Society had three stables in the City and he was still working with horses.

To a modern school leaver all this must seem a life of unendurable drudgery for a pittance, but the remarkable thing about Harry Plaxton is that, like many of his generation, he looks back, not with anger, but with pride and great good humour.

AN ISLAND OF TRANQUILLITY

Sunk Island

Sunk Island is a place which everyone has heard of but few have visited. The name is unforgettable but, it has to be admitted, Sunk Island is a long way from anywhere and there's no question of just passing through.

It is, however, a journey worth making and those who go for the first time are often pleasantly surprised. The land is flat and there are great skies overhead, but, rather than being overwhelmed by emptiness and isolation, most people experience a tranquil, soothing atmosphere, a haven of peace in a stress-ridden world.

Remarkably for such a remote place, Sunk Island has featured in the novels of two distinguished writers, and it has been well served by good historians, among them George de Boer and John Whitehead.

Hull-born Hubert Nicholson, who died a short time ago, knew the area intimately from childhood when his parents rented a holiday cottage in Holderness, and used the emotive title, *Sunk Island*, for his best-known book (published in 1956). He returned for a nostalgic visit when a new edition was issued in 1988.

It's still a good read, with echoes of Thomas Hardy in its story of farming families whose lives are no less dramatic for being lived far from the madding crowd, but for local people a particular interest is the accuracy with which Nicholson depicts the unique landscape. As one of the characters rode out from Ottringham he felt that 'this was the unseen frontier, the place where the normal, well-peopled countryside ended and the strange land began. After a kink or two, the lane opened out into the barest road in the East Riding, that looked as if it might run straight off the earth.'

Winifred Holtby was equally sensitive to the beguiling atmosphere of the Island, which appeared in her novel, *South Riding*, as the fictional Cold Harbour Colony, and one of her most poetic descriptions is of 'The wide Dutch landscape, haunted by larks and seabirds, roofed by immense pavilions of windy cloud; the miles of

Holy Trinity Church, Sunk Island.

19

brownish-purple shining mud, pocked and hummocked by water and fringed by heath-like herbs; the indented banks where the high tides sucked and gurgled.'

The rise of Sunk Island from the waters of the Humber is a saga of strenuous co-operation between Man and Nature. In recent years the focus has been on coastal erosion, but there have been gains as well as losses, and it was in the mid-16th century that the first sighting was made at low tide of a small island, known at first as Sunk Sands, which continued to grow and, being Crown Land, was leased to tenants who were required to embank. By the early 19th century it was attached to the mainland, and the opening in 1841 of the turnpiked road from Ottringham linked it firmly to the rest of Holderness.

This long, straight tree-lined road, described by Hubert Nicholson, seems longer every time you go along it, but eventually you do arrive at the nearest thing Sunk Island has to a centre, with its church, former school and village hall.

Another surprise is coming across such a fine and sophisticated piece of architecture as Holy Trinity Church in such a remote area. A chapel was erected at this spot in 1802 but by 1865 it was in poor repair. Accordingly, it was demolished and the present church, designed by the eminent architect, Ewan Christian, was built in 1876-7. Declared redundant in 1983, it now contains an excellent exhibition on the history of the Island and on Winifred Holtby. Although it is normally locked, don't despair and go away frustrated: the key can be obtained at any time from Mr. H. Ruddock at the Old Vicarage nearby.

OUT OF SCHOOL

School holidays in rural East Yorkshire

No one can ever be too old to forget how mounting excitement became almost unbearable as the summer term limped slowly on towards the day when you were released from the prison of school for what seemed endless weeks of freedom.

But people who were born at the turn of the 20th century or earlier would often refer to the summer holidays as the 'harvest holidays'. They remembered the time when the real reason for the long break was neither rest nor recreation but to avoid the mass absenteeism which would inevitably result when many children were needed to work in the fields.

The holiday usually started later than it does today because the intention was to coincide with the time when crops were ripe for harvesting. In 1877 the last day of term at Hedon School came on Friday, 17 August, and a four-week holiday began. Nature, however, takes no account of school timetables, and a month later, when the autumn term started on Monday, 17 September, there was a poor attendance 'owing to the harvest not being ended', and the problem persisted into the following week. Two years later the School Board, determined not to be caught out again, decided the holiday should not begin until 7 September.

But forecasting the weather is notoriously difficult and there was one year, 1896, when a fine spell led to an exceptionally early harvest. School began at Hedon as usual on Monday, 3 August, but the Board realised that farming and food must take priority over education. Orders were given to begin the harvest holiday without delay, and the scholars, as they were then called, assembled on Market Hill, and marched in fours to the Market Place where they were dismissed, all by half past nine.

The more rural a school the more calls there were

on children to leave their lessons and lend a hand. When Welwick School was re-opened on 1 October, 1889, only ten children attended: harvest operations were still not finished and many children were busy 'making bands in the fields or tending pigs in the fields of stubble', according to the log book edited , as a fascinating publication by Larry Malkin, Ann Stothard and Dorothy Smith under the title, *The Village of Welwick and its School*. On other occasions boys were absent 'singling' turnips, scaring birds, driving the horses, drilling seed, or potato picking. It is significant that an entry in 1909 reads: 'The farmers decided to fix the date for school closing: September 3rd.'

Easington in Times Past, by the same three authors, records a similar incident to the Hedon emergency. After a week of poor attendance with 'nearly all the absentees working on farms', the powers-that-be had to bow to the pressure of events, and at 11.30 a.m. on 13 August, 1915, Easington School began its harvest holiday.

The work was back-breaking and hands became calloused, but harvesting then was a social activity involving the whole community. Old photographs show people of every generation doing their bit, the complete opposite of today's picture of a solitary man on a machine in a prairie field.

And, during term, there were those golden days when 'something happened'. It could be an unofficial holiday when everybody wanted to join in the fun of the hirings or, in that pre-television age, when children stayed off school to see the arrival of the candidates in a general election.

Sometimes the holiday was approved when, for example, it celebrated one of Queen Victoria's Jubilees or the Relief of Mafeking. There were also important village events, such as the day in 1914 when the Wesleyan and Primitive School outings from Easington had as their destinations Withernsea and Holmpton – a day out which would stay as long and as lovingly in the memory as any package tour to Benidorm or Marbella.

THE ODD ISLAND OFF SPURN
Ravenser Odd

Spurn hangs on by the skin of its teeth, and, standing at the furthermost point, where the swirling waters of the Humber and the North Sea meet, you realise how incredible it is that such a place should ever exist.

It is even harder to believe that somewhere off the end of this precarious peninsula was once the flourishing island port of Ravenser Odd, a place which has interested me ever since I heard that charismatic historian, Ken MacMahon, lecture on the subject in one of the excellent classes he used to hold at Longcroft School.

There are references to this remote part of Holderness in the Norse sagas. The name, Ravenser, originally Hrafnseyri, means 'Raven's sandbank', and Spurn ('a projecting piece of land') completed the full name, Ravenser Spurn. The 'Raven' could refer to the bird, or even to someone's name, and Ken MacMahon aired another possibility: it might describe the raven-like appearance of this strip of land, curving like the beak of the predatory bird.

By the early 13th century the powerful thrust of the sea had broken through the fragile tip and formed the island of Ravenser Odd, connected to the mainland by the narrowest of sandy causeways covered with round yellow stones, which just managed to rise above the water so dangerously near on either side.

'Odd' means 'small point of land,' and on this most unlikely of sites a town was created. By 1280 it was big enough to cause problems to the men of Hedon, who complained that their own trade was being damaged by two rival ports, Ravenser Odd and Hull, where there were 'good harbours growing from day to day'. In 1299 it was granted its charter by Edward I and by 1305 it was sending two M.P.s to Westminster.

Re-creating the appearance of the town in the

absence of any pictures requires a considerable effort of imagination. We know, however, that it had a chapel of St. Mary, a street named Newgate, mills, a tan house, a twice-weekly market and an autumn fair. Fishing was a major activity, and from the Baltic and Low Countries came such varied cargoes as timber, fish, salt and tar. It was also conveniently placed for the locals to indulge in a little piracy.

Ravenser Odd's long-term survival was always chancy, and the beginning of the end was a period of severe storms and high tides which started around 1340. The quays were wrecked, their timber pillaged and the chapel ruined. According to the Chronicle of Meaux, 'the corpses and bones of the dead there buried horribly appeared', and, though one bell was sold to the mother church at Easington and two smaller bells to Aldbrough,

other items were appropriated by the irreligious. Within 20 years Ravenser Odd was abandoned.

A number of other villages in South Holderness also suffered in this period of ferocious storms and floods. There was Tharlesthorpe, with its meadows, cornfields and windmills and more than 1,000 sheep, pastured on such rich land that most ewes produced two lambs. Nearby was Frismarsh, and other strong-sounding names in the litany of lost villages: Pensthorpe, Orwithfleet, East Somert and Sunthorpe. All went the way of Ravenser Odd.

It's a sad story and unfortunately, not part of a long-dead history. Holderness is being eaten away at a rapid rate and the North Sea may ultimately wash up to the Wolds. 'And where exactly was Beverley?' historians of the future may one day ask.

Spurn lighthouse.

IN SEARCH OF MR. HUDSON

John Anthony Hudson of Longcroft Hall

Longcroft Hall is now occupied by Beverley College, but, like many official buildings, it began life as a private residence. Recently, I had a phone call from the College, asking if I could add to their information about the first man to live there, John Anthony Hudson. They already knew that he had bought The Lodge, at the bottom of Gallows Lane, in 1861, and there is at the College a sketch by his talented artist son, John Harold Hudson, but, apart from an unattributed statement that Hudson senior was 'a rich trawler owner', not much else.

History is the ideal subject for those who like detective problems. All investigators work from the basis of what is already known: in historical research this means starting with printed books as there's no point in retracing a route already taken by someone else. Phyl Frost's book, *Molescroft*, mentions that J. A. Hudson was the son of a Hull brickmaker, and the *Victoria County History* volume on Beverley states that the house, originally just called Longcroft, was built c1863 to the design of William Botterill of Hull.

At this stage it was important to see what information the staff of the Beverley Reference Library had already acquired about Hudson – quite a lot, in fact. Their indexes showed that he appeared in Beverley directories 1855-8 with an address in North Bar Without, and at Longcroft from the 1860s until his death. Starting at the end is another time-saving tip for researchers, as an obituary often gives a useful survey of a person's life. The Beverley librarians had photocopied the press report of Hudson's death, at the age of 86, in 1921, sub-titled 'A Veteran East Riding Magistrate'. He had, it stated, been appointed a J.P. in 1858, was Chairman of the North Hunsley Bench for many years, a staunch member of the Church of England, a trustee of the Minster Old Fund, and a strong Conservative. But, you will notice, no mention of the source of his wealth.

Another newspaper extract gave a splendidly detailed description of his marriage in 1856 to Adelaide Brereton, a doctor's daughter: 'As far as we know of the annals of Beverley, no wedding was ever celebrated in such a correct and imposing manner.' The groom rode to St. Mary's Church in a carriage specially made for the occasion, everyone admired the bride's 'jewelled bracelets which clasped her nicely rounded arms', and the happy couple had a two-month honeymoon touring the Continent.

Census records provide impressive evidence of the life-style enjoyed at Longcroft Hall. In 1871, the Hudsons had three children, a resident governess, butler, cook, housemaid, kitchenmaid and nursemaid, and Hudson himself, always described as 'J.P.', had the additional information, 'landowner', included in 1881, and 'living on own means' in 1891.

The reminiscences of a man familiar with the fine gardens of the area published in a magazine article include some interesting facts. Gallows Lane, then the drive to Longcroft Hall, had 'wonderful gardens alongside', and behind the wall, still there on the left, was the walled garden with its glasshouses, fruit and vegetables.

Hudson's place of birth was Dairycoates Grange. In the census of 1841 he appears there for the first time as a seven-year-old boy living with his father, John, a brick and tile maker. So far, however, I have been unable to substantiate the statement that Hudson was a trawler owner (there was a family of that name, probably unrelated, in the business), but Arthur Credland of the Maritime Museum suggests that he may have been an underwriter, one of the financiers who kept very much in the background.

The story is by no means complete. Far more is known about the man who succeeded the Hudsons at Longcroft Hall, Gordon Armstrong – but that could be for another time.

ALL EYES WERE ON WITHERNSEA
Church Bazaar, 1858

Withernsea was the place where everyone wanted to be on Wednesday, 4 August 1858. Each hour a special train took hundreds more passengers to swell the crowds, and, even though extra carriages had been added to create trains 'of almost unexampled length', many would-be travellers were left behind when it became impossible to squeeze another one on board. Most of the passengers were 'gaily dressed ladies', and the scene at Withernsea, according to an enthusiastic reporter, was 'really stirring'.

And the reason for all the excitement? A church bazaar – a function which today would barely raise more than a glimmer of interest. Our Victorian ancestors, however, with neither radio nor television on tap, never lost an opportunity for a good day out, and this bazaar was something out of the ordinary.

Withernsea had come into existence as a seaside resort only four years previously, when it was selected as the terminal point of the Hull and Holderness Railway in preference to Easington or Tunstall. Merely 'a long, straggling village on the sea cliff' until that time, it was in the process of being transformed into what the press described as 'the New Brighton of Hull', with a fine hotel (later the convalescent home, but now demolished) designed by the eminent architect, Cuthbert Brodrick, and with builders responding so eagerly to the inducements of the railway directors that – a slight exaggeration here – they had seen 'the present handsome village spring up almost by magic, and which by daily extension and rising favour is shortly to assume a very important position among our English watering places'.

There was one glaring omission from this promising scenario. St. Nicholas Church was in a sorry state. Consecrated in 1488, it had lost its roof in 1609 during a terrible storm, and, ever since, it had been left to fall into ruin. No self-respecting Victorian resort could be without adequate 'church accommodation', and so, although there were opponents who thought 'its rent tower, tottering pillars, crumbling arches and grass-covered aisles' too picturesque to alter, it was decided to begin immediate restoration.

Brodrick was employed as architect, and scaffolding was erected round the walls but there was an urgent need to raise money. 'In a happy moment some individual suggested a bazaar', and there was the firm intention that this was to be an event to remember.

A spacious dancing saloon in the pleasure ground near the hotel was the venue, and the reporter who described the splendour of the scene was determined that none of his readers who had failed to attend should be left in any doubt of the delights they had missed. Flags and flowers were everywhere and no superlative was spared. A galaxy of leaders of local society graced the bazaar with their presence, and the impressive list, packed with famous names, is proof of the interest they took in Withernsea in those early halcyon days.

The bazaar continued into the Thursday, the sun shone, and it was all a brilliant success, with £281 raised the first day and £200 the second. There was also one significant difference from modern crowd-pulling events. 'A strong body of police' was in attendance, but so well-behaved was everyone that their work 'on this occasion was a perfect sinecure'.

A 'PEASE' OF LOCAL HISTORY

Joseph Robinson Pease

Hesslewood Hall and the Pease family, its original occupants, were the subject of a letter I recently received from Ireland. The writer, now 90, explained that her grandmother was Annie Sarah Pease, the elder daughter of a Mr. Pease (Christian name unknown), the second son of Joseph Robinson Pease of Hesslewood. This was all the information which had come down to her, and, understandably, she was interested in learning something more about her grandmother's family.

The Peases were important and influential people in their heyday whom most of us would be happy to have as ancestors, but over the generations large families tend to grow apart, and those descended from a second son are likely to lose their links with the senior branch of the family. Give a few generations and it's quite easy to see how knowledge of one's distinguished forebears can become rather sketchy.

The central building, No. 12 Charlotte Street: the town residence of J. R. Pease.

J. R. Pease, as depicted in the volume of his diaries, The Journal of Joseph Robinson Pease, 1822-1865
(East Yorkshire Local History Society, 2000).

The Joseph Robinson Pease at the heart of the lady's query was the one who had Hesslewood Hall built in 1783 to the design of a distinguished Hull architect, Charles Mountain, as a replacement for the original, more modest family home there. His plan was to use it as his summer villa, with picturesque views of the Humber and the ships passing by, and at the same time he commissioned Mountain to design him a town house in Charlotte Street, the most fashionable address in Georgian Hull. The Pease house was No. 12, the finest, central house in a very impressive terrace fronting the street, and it was there he could escape the cold winter winds blowing across the Humber.

These projects cost money – £20,000 for the Charlotte Street terrace, £4,000 for Hesslewood, and £5,000 for furnishing the two houses – but J. R. Pease was a man of means. When only 26 he had inherited vast wealth on the death of his 90-year-old grandfather, Joseph, whose money came from a commercial empire which included shipping, whaling and oil crushing, and, most celebrated of all his activities, Hull's first bank, founded in 1754 and known locally as the Old Bank.

J. R. Pease was particularly fortunate to be the sole heir of grandfather Joseph, who left no immediate male descendants to carry on his multifarious activities, only a daughter, Mary. She married a Manchester merchant, Robert Robinson and their only son to survive childhood, Joseph Robinson, was consequently in line to inherit his grandfather's fortune. At the age of 21 he changed his surname to Pease, and in 1778, as Joseph Robinson Pease, became the head of the family and a powerful figure in business and banking, with the resources to build large residences appropriate to a man of his importance.

Eldest sons in the past tended to take the lion's share of the family inheritance, and it was Joseph Robinson Pease's first-born son of identical name, who at the age of 17 succeeded him in 1807, leaving his younger brother, Clifford, and his descendants (among them the grandmother of the lady who wrote to me) to go their separate ways.

Families, like nations, rise and fall. Later generations of Peases had less commercial clout and in 1921 Hesslewood Hall began a new phase of life as the Hull Seamen's and General Orphanage. Later it became an hotel and is now professional offices.

The house in Charlotte Street was demolished in 1969, but two Pease warehouses of 1745 and 1760, now converted into apartments, still stand beside the River Hull, and the city where they wielded such power still has its Pease Street.

LOST GARDENS

Botanic Gardens, Spring Bank West

Botanic Gardens, for those whose memories go back at least to 1964, was a suburban station on the Hornsea and Withernsea lines, now merely the 'crossing' where three busy roads meet, without the clanging gates which barred the way at the most inconvenient times and caused an army of frustrated cyclists to charge forward the very second they were opened.

The nearby Botanic Gardens had closed years before, but the name was a reminder of an ambitious scheme to provide the town with attractive, well-planned grounds where visitors could promenade on five acres of open lawn, stroll by a lake, listen to the band, and, on Monday evenings in the summer, marvel at the fireworks.

These Botanic Gardens, off Spring Bank West, were not the first in Hull. Earlier ones on Anlaby Road had been opened on 6 June 1812 with a lecture from the President, Dr. John Alderson, on the progress and advantages of botanical knowledge, and his statue now stands outside the Hull Royal Infirmary looking across the road towards the former site of the six-acre gardens, still marked by Linnaeus Street, named after the Swedish botanist.

They sound an idyllic spot where, on Sundays, select parties spent many pleasant hours 'beneath the old oak, listening to the warble of the birds and enjoying the cool shades', but there was no question of free admission to all and sundry. The gardens were not a public park, but strictly the preserve of subscribers, so exclusive that nursemaids in charge of members' children were not deemed fit to enter. It was a fashionable organisation and the local press reported its affairs, giving particular prominence to the gifts of important people who donated seeds brought from distant parts of the world.

So elitist were the gardens that they excluded the numbers needed to bring in enough income. It was not until the highly talented 35-year-old James Craig Niven was appointed Curator in 1853 that their management was improved, with the membership list trebling and the collection of plants developed as one of the finest in the country.

The growing prosperity of Hull, however, ironically blighted their existence. Originally on the outskirts, they became stranded in an increasingly built-up area as the spreading town ate up more and more land. Trees and plants inevitably suffered from pollution, and the decision was taken to move to a larger site with much greater potential in Spring Bank West.

In 1877 the old gardens were closed, but continuity was maintained by Niven remaining as Curator. He was a landscape gardener of outstanding ability who had designed Pearson Park and the terraced gardens of Brantinghamthorpe, and he approached this new challenge with imagination and enthusiasm. A three-acre lake, with a windmill on a central island, was 'surrounded by a bank of rhododendrons and other showy plants', a large ornamental fountain and a band stand were focal points, and a semi-circle of flower beds was to be overlooked by a raised terrace of glasshouses.

Not surprisingly, it was not all completed in time for the official opening on 19 July 1880, though a more immediate concern was the appalling weather. Children from the Spring Bank Orphanage set out in procession but, as a reporter with no sense of humour recorded, 'Before they arrived at the gates the rain began to fall heavily, which somewhat accelerated their movements and rendered the scene less imposing.'

Dr. R. M. Craven declared the new gardens open but, with typical Victorian earnestness, reminded his audience that the study of botany was more important than 'mere pleasure and amusement'. Even so, they were the scene of elegant social occasions which reached their peak in 1882 with the planting of two trees by the Duke of Edinburgh, son of Queen Victoria.

Sadly, Niven did not live to see the realisation of his dreams. A workaholic who overtaxed his strength, he had been in poor health for some time and died, though still 'in harness', in October 1881. The gardens, too, did not enjoy the long future they deserved. Free public parks were now a powerful threat to private gardens and the opening of West Park, not far away, in 1885 was another reason for taking one's leisure in a place where there were no admission charges.

In 1890 the gardens closed, but there was a final stroke of luck. The site was ideal for the new Hymers College, opened in 1893, and it remains a green oasis surrounded by fine trees and with a part of the lake still visible. And in a dry summer the outline of the bandstand appears in the grass, a silent reminder of past glories.

A posed picture at the lake of the former Botanic Gardens.

MEN OF POWER IN THE NORTH

The Percy family of Wressle and Leconfield

Wressle Castle, even in its ruined state, is an impressive sight in an area where castles are not thick on the ground. Proof, too, of the importance of its owners, members of the Percy family who were a power in the North of England, and, from 1377, Earls of Northumberland.

It was built in 1380, a massive four-sided stone edifice surrounding a central courtyard, in its heyday at the turn of the 16th century, in the time of the 5th Earl (always known as 'The Magnificent'). Thereafter

it was downhill all the way, gradual at first, but dramatic in 1650, when three-quarters of the huge complex were demolished by the Parliamentarians to prevent its use by their Royalist opponents in the Civil War. What remained was converted into a farmhouse, and even that suffered further degradation when its still fine interior was gutted by fire in 1796.

The ruins of once great buildings have their own distinctive character as visual reminders of the fragile nature of all earthly power, and there's certainly more

Wressle Castle.

to see at Wressle than at the other Percy stronghold in the East Riding, Leconfield.

A right of way on the left-hand side of the village as you travel from Beverley leads to the site of the moated Leconfield Castle, another four-sided complex with a central courtyard, but, unlike Wressle, built of wood, apart from one side which was brick and stone. Hollows in the ground are all your imagination has to help it re-create the great aristocratic residence (far bigger than Wressle and with twice the number of rooms) which stood in this quiet spot among the trees.

The famous *Northumberland Household Book* gives details of the establishment here and at Wressle, at their peak around 1512, when jointly they employed 166 servants in this last flaunt of medieval splendour. After the Gunpowder Plot of 1605 came accusations of involvement in an act of treason, and land was sold to pay an onerous fine of £30,000. Leconfield Castle was demolished and some of its fittings removed to Wressle, which still had a few years to go.

The family had strong links with Beverley, and the Minster has its Percy Chapel and its Percy Tomb. In the Chapel is the tomb of the 4th Earl, who in 1489 was killed by a mob at Topcliffe near Thirsk, but who had the consolation of a splendid funeral in Beverley. Not far away, however, is the memorial known as the Percy Tomb or Shrine, a most daring example of ornate stone carving and an artistic treasure of national importance.

Ironically, no one is certain whom it honours. It could be Lady Eleanor Percy, who died in 1328, but Lady Idonea has also been suggested. Two Beverley men of the early 19th century had no interest in the identity of the deceased when they decided to rob the tomb under the mistaken belief that it contained a corpse buried with £80,000 worth of jewellery. Somehow, they managed to enter the Minster at night and removed the top stone, unaware that they were being watched by the sexton, who appears to have known about the intended crime. He went to call out the organist, George Lambert, and together they entered the church. Lambert took his seat, with the sexton at the bellows, and suddenly 'the organ sent forth a most bellowing sound', terrifying the robbers, who let the stone fall and break, and rushed out, abandoning their tools. It was an act of disrespect which the Earls of Northumberland would have handled very differently.

A STREET TO STAND AND STARE
Whitefriargate, Hull

Whitefriargate will always be 'Whitefr'argate' to local people, forever remembered as the liveliest street in Hull, solid with shoppers on Saturday afternoons, and with cars nudging dangerously through the human tide.

Originally it was merely a section of the longer Aldgate, which included Scale Lane and Silver Street and ran east to west through medieval Hull. The part later called Whitefriargate took its name from the white-robed Carmelite friars, who had arrived in Hull by 1289 and who moved in 1304 to a three-acre site on the southern side of the street. In 1539, at the dissolution of the monasteries, their property passed to lay owners and in 1621 it was granted by Thomas Ferries to Trinity House.

The familiar facades of the country's leading chain stores have robbed town centres of much of their individuality – but only at street level. Look above and you see a different world where upper storeys survive unchanged. Fortunately, standing and staring is far less hazardous than it was before pedestrianisation in 1975.

The finest buildings are those on the southern side, where Trinity House has had the means to develop their site on an impressive scale and to proclaim their ownership with nautical symbols and their motto packed with meaning: *Spes super sidera*: Hope beyond the stars. Above Poundstretcher are the two upper storeys of the former Smith's Bank. During construction, 1829-30, human bones and skulls were discovered, an indication that this was probably the friars' burial ground, and placed in the crypt of St. Charles Church. Further along is an archway where, peering through a gate, you get a partial glimpse of a more modest but still important building which started life as a Post Office in 1843 and later became Humber Conservancy Buildings.

But grandest of all are the premises now occupied by Boots, the former Neptune Inn, intended to be Hull's smartest hotel when it was built , 1794-7, soon after the opening of the first dock (now the site of Queens Gardens). An equally elegant Parliament Street was opened as a link from the Old Town to the dock and the new suburbs beyond, and from the sumptuous ballroom on the first floor affluent guests could look along this new street and see the ships which brought wealth to Hull. For reasons which are not quite clear, maybe the drinker's traditional loyalty to his usual hostelry, in 1815 the Neptune became Hull's Custom House.

Georgian architecture is not short of admirers, but that's no reason to undervalue the best of what followed. We can now appreciate the proud Victorian buildings, once dismissed as ostentatious, and Whitefriargate has some good examples on its northern side, particularly the Midland Bank, designed like an Italian palazzo.

The 1930s were a time when the centre of Hull was becoming increasingly stylish, and the 1934 building now occupied by Superdrug and Adams Childrenswear is redolent of that period. The 'six giant fluted columns' of Marks and Spencer's (1931) are worth more than a passing glance, but surely surpassing all Hull's buildings of that decade is Burton Menswear, opened 4 December 1936 by Montague Burton's son, Stanley, who claimed that he 'did not know a site so well placed in England as this one'.

And, even after this rich medley there are the foundations of Beverley Gate, the main entrance to the walled town, where, on one of the great occasions of English history, Charles I was denied entry in 1642. It was a refusal which lost him more than the chance to ride down Whitefriargate.

Beverley Gate at the entrance to Whitefriargate.

SEASON OF MISTS AND . . . CONKERS

Children's Games

'Hull Fair weather' comes at the 'back end of the year' when 'the nights are drawing in': three emotive ways of referring to autumn, the time when Bonfire Night and its horrid American import, 'trick or treat', are on the horizon, though Hull schoolchildren no longer have the traditional holiday on 4 December, Town Taking Day, to celebrate the rising of 1688 when supporters of the future William III captured the Catholic governor of the town, Lord Langdale, and gained possession of the Citadel.

An autumn ritual still observed as vigorously as ever is the fierce fighting between the owners of rival conkers, and I've recently been interested to read some memoirs written by Bill Hope, of Molescroft, formerly Secretary of Hull Chamber of Commerce, who comments that: 'Most children's games before the war were markedly seasonal in character.' There seemed to be a mysterious subculture in which information was transmitted instantaneously through the City's schools so that every child changed to a new pastime on the same day.

According to Bill Hope, the yearly cycle began around Easter, when tops and skipping ropes were the craze, some of the ropes being 'quite lengthy, reaching from one side of the road to the other'. One striking difference from today was that so many games could take place in the street – in perfect safety. 'The only vehicles using the side streets,' he writes, 'were the occasional dustcarts, furniture pantechnicons (people always seemed to be on the move) and tradesmen's vans. In the twenties and early thirties all of these were invariably horse-drawn.'

I have been told that earlier this century a schoolmaster in Thorngumbald let his pupils out to spend playtime on the road, now the busy route from Hull to Withernsea, and older people sometimes look back with amazement at the freedom possible when they were young. In the holidays they spent whole days outside, unsupervised, and with parents apparently unworried. My mother and her brothers and sisters, who lived at Little Humber, spent a lot of time on the river bank, inviting their friends for a picnic and boiling a kettle on a fire they made from wood left behind by the tide.

Bill Hope lived as a boy in Cambridge Grove, East Hull, and there were still open fields nearby which were adopted as unofficial playgrounds. Another amenity was the Marfleet Drain, a favourite venue for fishing and swimming. It was, he points out, 'much cleaner in terms of pollution than many natural rivers would be today'. Some of his schoolfriends swam there regularly, and, as far as he can recall, 'came to no particular harm'.

Each year there was a short season of 'piggy', a game known elsewhere in Yorkshire as knurr and spell, and spring was the season for hoops, which ranged from superior wooden versions purchased by the fortunate minority to redundant bike wheels, called 'boolers' if they were complete with tyres and spokes. Some games, such as leap frog and block, required no equipment but plenty of energy, and there was a particularly tough one Bill disliked which had the warning name of 'ton weight coming on heavy'.

Altogether gentler was collecting cigarette cards, a painless way of absorbing knowledge, though boys who found this too tame invented games which required the ability to flick cards long distances with perfect accuracy.

In an age of computers and Internet these are memories worth preserving.

THE BEGINNING OF THE LINE

Opening of the Bridlington railway, 1846

Bridlington.

Recent good news about the future of the Hull-Bridlington railway will probably arouse as much pleasure as the opening of the line 150 years ago, on 6 October 1846. Missing, though, is any sign of the excitement and enthusiasm which marked this new example of Victorian enterprise.

Well before opening day local people were keenly watching activities on the line. Towards the end of February work was 'rapidly progressing in the neighbourhood of Beverley' and exciting 'a good deal of interest', not least because of difficulties which threatened completion. The contractors were struggling to get a solid foundation in a field in Beverley Parks and several men were pumping and baling out water all day and night, though without apparent success.

At Driffield, however, the news was much brighter. Work was going ahead at full speed, with King's Beck 'forded by a viaduct of four arches', and on a remarkably fine Sunday nearly the whole of Driffield turned out for their first-ever view of a railway. Church and chapel attendances suffered in consequence and one minister upbraided those delinquents whose curiosity had led them into such sinful ways on the Sabbath. But the long-awaited day finally came, and at 10 past 11 on 6 October (already 40 minutes late) a massive train of 66 carriages pulled by three engines, the Aerial, Hudson and Antelope, left Hull Station (then near Humber Dock). Torrents of rain soaked spectators waiting by the track, but nothing could detract from the 'very beautiful appearance' of the train as it came into view.

There was a stop at Cottingham, and at Beverley and Driffield where large crowds applauded and bands played as the train arrived. At Bridlington, journey's end, an amazing 900 enjoyed a sumptuous luncheon in the goods station, presided over by the Railway King himself, George Hudson, then M.P. for Sunderland as well as Chairman of the York and North Midland Railway. It was a day for self-congratulation, untroubled by any disclosures of the financial manoeuvrings which would end his career in disgrace. Hudson was not lost for words as he confidently prophesied that the line would 'promote commercial prosperity' and 'provide the means for the health and he hoped also for the long life of thousands of persons residing in that district'.

The station had, as a compromise, been built halfway between Bridlington Town and the port area, Bridlington Quay, which developed into the seaside resort. Visitors unfortunately tend to regard this as the whole of Bridlington and neglect the Old Town with its Priory and its fascinating High Street, one of the finest Georgian streets in the country.

At about 3.30 pm the train returned to Hull, with more auspicious weather bringing out bigger crowds. The celebrations were far from over and a distinguished company of around 340 sat down in the Public Rooms, Jarratt Street, to another magnificent spread. Once again Hudson treated them to an orgy of oratory: as he had to work his way through a list of no fewer than 21 toasts, and he and many of his friends wanted to return to York that night, he regretted having to perform these formalities rather rapidly. There was a slight contretemps when the Chairman of the Hull Dock Company took umbrage at an insinuation that the port facilities were inadequate and impeding growth, but more honeyed words and more drinks helped calm ruffled tempers, and Hudson and his party left for York at midnight.

Luckily the line had been opened in time for Hull Fair, and the following week Beverley station 'presented a busy scene' as more than 1,000 took advantage of bargain-price tickets. So great was the demand in Driffield that carriages were filled to overcrowding, some even attempted to scramble on the top of coaches, and crowds at stations along the way were left behind.

Who says that the Victorians didn't know how to enjoy themselves?

SAME PLACE, DIFFERENT PROGRAMME

Hull's Assembly Rooms

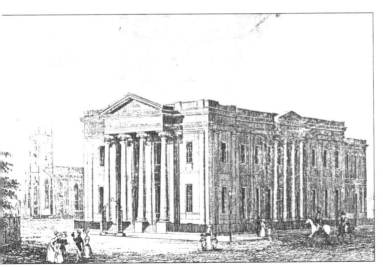

'Does anyone know what happened to a building in Hull which was originally the Assembly Rooms?' was a query to the East Yorkshire Family History Society from a member in Leeds whose grandfather was manager there at the turn of the century. The answer, as many already know, is that it survives on its prominent site at the corner of Kingston Square and Jarratt Street, but now enjoying a renaissance as the New Theatre.

Hull had had assembly rooms at various places where affluent residents gathered for their great social events, but in 1827 there was a strong feeling that the town deserved something more appropriate to its 'rank and opulence'. At a meeting held in the Guildhall on 22 February that year, John Broadley, a member of a leading local family, put the unanswerable case for undertaking such a

Assembly Rooms; Christ Church – left.

project. The (still flourishing) Literary and Philosophical Society had no suitable room in which to hold its lectures, nowhere to keep its museum or art collection: 'It was a disgrace to Hull that, if any matter occurred, there was no place in which to assemble and consult upon it.' A similar theme linked other speeches. The town, said Rev. J. H. Bromby, Vicar of Holy Trinity, was 'lifting up its head', not only equal but 'ever superior to many of its neighbours'.

Soon afterwards an advertisement for a suitable site appeared in the local press. A month later it was announced that a plot had been selected, and an appeal was made for gentlemen subscribers to support the venture; over £8,000 had already been collected towards the £10,000 needed.

But it was July 1830 before the foundation stone was laid, and 1834 before work was completed. It was, nevertheless, a building worth waiting for, with its great portico of Ionic columns which have survived conversion to the New Theatre. The interior was equally grand. A suite of smart apartments, music room, drawing room and dining room occupied the ground floor, and upstairs was the spacious lecture room.

The Assembly Rooms (or Public Rooms, as they were usually called) rapidly became the principal venue for important public functions. I have already mentioned the dinner held there in 1846 to celebrate the opening of the Hull-Bridlington railway, and in the same year a grand ball, held at the Public Rooms under the patronage of Lady Clifford Constable, 'was numerously and fashionably attended'.

Political meetings brought in far bigger and more enthusiastic audiences than they would today, and as well as the serious stuff there were the pre-poll 'breakfasts' and the celebratory dinners of the victorious candidates. In 1852, for example, Sheriff Harrison hosted a meal which 'consisted of every requisite which at such a repast could either please the eye or delight the palate', with such delicacies as strawberries, grapes, dressed fruit and champagne. On three occasions Charles Dickens enthralled audiences

in the Public Rooms with his mesmeric readings. In a changing world, the premises were licensed as a cinema.

The transformation into the New Theatre came in 1939. An old lecture hall next door had, in 1924, been turned into the Little Theatre, which established a high reputation with performances by a galaxy of young actors who later became famous. A newly appointed, charismatic manager, Peppino Santangelo, saw the adjacent Assembly Rooms, still used for dances, as a building with more potential, and an exchange of property with Hull Corporation took place, though the outbreak of war in 1939 threatened to put a damper on the New Theatre before it had even had a chance to show its paces. On 16 October, however, it was able to open with a production of *Me and My Girl*. Not exactly what the founding fathers had in mind in 1827.

'CALL ME SIR, NOT MADAM'
Prominent Women

Amy Johnson needs no introduction, but individual women receive relatively few mentions in local history.

Our knowledge of the past depends so much on the records which survive. As public life and business were male preserves, it is the names of prominent men which are kept alive – though one name in the famous Hull firm, Rose, Down and Thompson, is that of a woman, Mrs. Christina Rose. Usually, though, the women whose work was so essential and who had such a profound influence on husbands and children remain anonymous.

Just a few emerge from obscurity in the early church in Yorkshire, like Abbesses Heraburga of Watton and Hilda of Whitby, and, coming down from those lofty

*Madame
Clapham.*

heights to a rough diamond in more recent times, a woman whose physical strength was more than equal to any male's was Rose Carr, the Hornsea carrier and carriage proprietor.

But there were many who were forceful figures in their immediate circles and who deserve a bigger share of the historical spotlight than they have so far received. What about the mother of William Crosskill, the pioneering Beverley agricultural engineer, who was left with seven children when her whitesmith husband died in 1812? She gamely carried on the business with the help of the eldest, the 12-year-old William, and gave

him the start which enabled him to become the town's leading industrialist.

Many will have sweet or sour memories of schoolmistresses of great character who were dominating figures in the lives of their pupils. When money became available for building what is now Hymers College, two teachers, Janet and Christina Bremner, put up a powerful case for opening the new school to girls as well as boys. Their sensible argument was dismissed as an absurd 'fad', yet history has given them the last laugh: in 1989 the school became co-educational.

Even such a chauvinistically male establishment as Hymers College had a small number of women on the staff, and most unforgettable of all was the art mistress, Mrs. Eileen Anderson, a tiny but forceful silver-haired, blue-rinsed figure, who insisted on being addressed as 'sir'. And at the Training College on Cottingham Road was the splendidly named Principal, Miss Cumberbirch. One of my own teachers, who was at the College during her reign, was almost expelled when she questioned the rule that no student should go into the town centre alone. 'But do you not realise that Hull is a sea port?' thundered Miss Cumberbirch.

Music and drama are other areas where talented women have earned a measure of fame, and a local book, *The Swelling Scene* ★, pays tribute to such stalwarts as Hannchen Drasdo, Phyllis Sharrah and Stella Sizer-Simpson, whose names still evoke nostalgic sighs.

But, apart from wonderful Amy, no one has surpassed the celebrity status of Madame Clapham who, as the simply named 'Mrs. Emily Clapham, Dressmaker', opened her business at No 1 Kingston Square in 1887 and who achieved the impossible by making Hull a centre of fashion. So successful was she that she expanded into two adjacent properties, promoted herself to the rank of 'Madame Clapham, Costumier', and acquired a glittering clientele which included the Wilson ladies of Tranby Croft and Warter Priory and Lady Ida Sitwell of Scarborough. By far her most important customer was Queen Maud of Norway, whose status demanded that

Madame Clapham visit her. Consequently the Queen never saw the luxurious showroom in Kingston Square. Nor did she see the spartan conditions in which the seamstresses (150 at the peak of the business) worked in bare and bitterly cold rooms.

Madame Clapham has earned the reputation of a dictatorial employer whose word was law and whose temper was legendary, but at least she is remembered, unlike a contemporary who has not been given her due recognition. In 1907 Mrs. C. Richardson was Hull's first woman candidate in a municipal election and yet, even with the help of Hull's excellent Local Studies Library, I've so far been unable to discover her Christian name.

The Swelling Scene, compiled by Pamela Dellar and Gillian Holtby, ed. Barbara Robinson (Highgate of Beverley 1996).

STAIRWAYS TO PROSPERITY
The Merchant Houses of High Street, Hull

High Street is a surprise to first-time visitors to Hull. They arrive expecting a stereotyped northern industrial city of factories set in a desert of dreariness. Instead, they find a narrow street echoing with history as their feet feel the gentle springing of its wooden setts.

One of its great delights, particularly for photographers, are the intriguing views along alleys and staithes towards the river which brought it into being. This is the birthplace of Hull, its first street, which grew up on the bank of the waterway where all the shipping of the port was concentrated. It still winds leisurely along, following the course of the river, though infilling over the centuries has moved it further inland.

In two world wars it has suffered grievously, but enough survives for anyone with an ounce of imagination to capture the atmosphere of the street, at its peak of prosperity in the 18th century. The annual midsummer weekend of open houses proves year after year that there are still local people who have never been inside No 160, Maister House, and seen its magnificent staircase, one of the artistic glories of Yorkshire. This was the house which the Maisters, a wealthy and powerful merchant family, rebuilt after a disastrous fire in 1743 in which Mrs. Henry Maister, her baby son, Nathaniel, and two maidservants lost their lives.

Maister House drawn by Francis Johnson (from the cover of Jennifer Rowley's House of Maister, *published by Hedon and Distrct Local History Society).*

Like all merchants' houses it served a dual purpose, and the ground floor rooms were the business offices. From the front door the staircase is invisible, and appears in all its splendour only when you walk down

A lost view of Wilberforce House (r) and the Georgian Houses (l).

At the northern end of the street, near the spot where the North Gate of the walled town once stood, is Blaydes House (No 6), the home and business premises of another important family. The Maritime Historical Studies Centre of Hull University, it has, behind its imposing door, a marble-floored entrance hall and a richly carved staircase, carefully calculated to impress potential customers with the solidity of the Blaydes' business as merchants and shipbuilders.

Quite apart from the grandeur of Blaydes House, obvious from its exterior, this is a part of High Street where you become very conscious of its long history. One ship built by the Blaydes, the *Bethia*, later had its name changed to Bounty, and achieved international fame after its crew took part in a mutiny. Number 1 nearby was the home of Sir Samuel Standidge, a power in the 18th-century port and host to royalty.

Towards the southern end of the street is Crowle House (No 41), not as well-known as the others because it's in a courtyard and is reached only through a passageway. But it has an impressive frontage with classical decoration and initials and a date commemorating George Crowle and his wife.

Altogether, with its museums and pubs full of character, this is a street for tourists to rave about and for local people to re-rediscover.

the hall and turn a corner. At this point Maister House becomes a home, with the stairs leading to the family apartments above. Gazing up through the well of the staircase is a visual experience more effective than any history book in its stunning evidence of the prosperity and level of taste in Georgian Hull.

The merchants' houses of High Street are rather like local people: plain on the outside but with all their riches within, ready to be revealed to those who take the trouble to look. Wilberforce House (No 25) has a sensible but unostentatious appearance, yet in its elegant hall is another fine staircase, richly carved and sweeping grandly upwards, with a unique source of added beauty, a delicately decorated ceiling which one writer has compared to a jeweller's snuff box.

GUY'S FRIENDS FROM HOLDERNESS
Welwick links with Guy Fawkes

The Gunpowder Plot has a particular interest for people in this area because two local men, John and Christopher Wright of Welwick, were involved. Yet, disappointingly, East Yorkshire receives no mention in Antonia Fraser's otherwise excellent and well illustrated book, *The Gunpowder Plot* (Weidenfeld & Nicolson, £20).

John and Christopher Wright (according to Antonia Fraser, always known as Jack and Kit) had their roots firmly set in Holderness as the sons of Robert and Ursula Wright of Ploughland Hall, Welwick. This was Robert's second marriage, and one of the many interesting features of the village church is a memorial brass to William Wright and his wife, Ann. The William commemorated was another of Robert's sons, by his first wife, Ann Grimston of Grimston Garth, and so half-brother to the two conspirators.

John was born in 1568 and Christopher two years later into a family with a Catholic background at a time when attendance on Sundays at the reformed Church of England was compulsory and fines were imposed on absentees. Some of the Wrights were probably among those who obeyed the letter of the law and kept their beliefs to themselves, but one who would not compromise with her conscience was John and Christopher's mother, who as a consequence spent

St. Mary's Church, Welwick.

many years in prison in Hull for refusing to attend a Protestant service.

After their early life in a home which must have left a deep impression on young boys, John and Christopher received an education which was another key factor in their story. They were sent to St. Peter's School, York, where a fellow pupil was Guy Fawkes. All three came under the influence of the Headmaster, John Pulleine, who outwardly conformed in order to keep his job but whose sympathies were with the old religion.

The Wrights had another family link with the

Gunpowder Plot. John and Christopher had a sister Martha, who had married Thomas Percy, a second cousin of the Earl of Northumberland, and, although he abandoned Martha, who was left to earn her living by teaching, this did not disrupt his relationship with his brothers-in-law. He was also to join in the plot.

History isn't always fair. Although Guy Fawkes takes all the blame because he was the one discovered and arrested in the cellar underneath the House of Lords, the real leader was Robert Catesby. Once the plot had been uncovered, the two Wright brothers and Thomas Percy escaped to Holbeach House, Staffordshire, but their attempt to barricade themselves inside was short-lived. Three were killed in the shooting which began when government forces arrived and when John Wright's renowned swordsmanship was no defence against guns.

Some traditions lapse after a time, but from the beginning the Gunpowder Plot has stirred popular imagination and bonfires have been lit ever since. Well into the 19th century it was still a day marked by religious services and the ringing of church bells. In 1850 a sermon specially adapted for the occasion was preached by the Rev. John Scott at St. John the Evangelist's Church (where the Ferens Art Gallery now stands), and a fireworks display ended with the singing of *Rule Britannia* and the National Anthem. In Beverley the annual fete was held at the Grammar School, where 'a large concourse of ladies and gentlemen' watched the burning of the Guy in a tar-tub on the bonfire. At Driffield things were not so orderly: a throng of disorderly young fellows began setting off fireworks in the street and the police had all their work cut out to keep order. Not quite the good old days.

QUEEN VICTORIA SLEPT HERE

The Visit of Queen Victoria, 1854

Kingston upon Hull may be its official title but, as far as names go, the city is very much a Queen's town. Queens Gardens, Queen's Road, Queen Victoria Square, Victoria Avenue, Victoria Pier and Victoria Street, along with Albert Avenue, Albert Dock and Prince's Dock, are all evidence of the impact made by Queen Victoria on her never-to-be forgotten visit in 1854 when, as a young wife and mother she was accompanied by her beloved Consort and five children.

The visit had been expected the previous year and it was fortunate that some preliminary work had been started then as it was only on 5 October 1854 that news was received that eight days later the Royal Family would stop off in Hull on their return journey from Balmoral to London. What was ever more exciting was the announcement that the Queen proposed to stay overnight, and the directors of the NER were quick to 'put at her disposal' the entire facilities of the Station Hotel.

To read the contemporary reports of the visit is to recapture something of the euphoria which spread through the town. 'In a few short hours the clink of the hammer and the harsh grinding of the saw said how busily all were engaged.' Streets were re-paved, buildings painted, barricades and triumphal arches erected for the royal progress through the streets, as well as a grandstand at the Pier where the Queen would embark in the royal yacht for a circumnavigation of the town docks.

At 6.00 pm on Friday, 13 October, the Mayor and Corporation, resplendent in robes, processed to Paragon Station, where privileged 'well-dressed gentlemen and ladies' were ranged in tiered ranks, and the band of the 7th Hussars and the Vocal Society were poised to burst into the National Anthem at the appropriate signal from the conductor's baton.

Tension rose as telegraphic messages told of the imminent approach of the royal train. At 4.59 it left Selby, at 5.08 Howden, and soon 'the ringing of a bell announced the arrival of Her Majesty'. Leaning on the arm of Prince Albert and followed by her children and an entourage which included the Prime Minister, Lord Aberdeen, she walked along the platform with the Mayor, Dr. Henry Cooper, and entered the hotel. In a magnificent throne room loyal addresses were presented to the Queen and Prince, though, mercifully, at her own request, they were not read aloud.

Official public ceremony was now over for the day and the Queen was left to enjoy the amenities of the hotel, where enormous trouble had been taken to show that Hull, which in 1642 had rebuffed Charles I, the last reigning monarch to visit the town, had made amends for its former slight. Sir Clifford Constable had lent his gold and silver plate and Trinity House some of its pictures, while floral decorations had been entrusted to James Niven, the talented curator of the Botanic Gardens.

Serenading Queen Victoria with the National Anthem.

And yet, amid all this splendour, it was stressed that the Queen preferred simplicity. Although a state bed had been provided for the Prince of Wales, a countermanding order stated that the children should have only camp beds, and the grander version was allocated to a governess. The following day, Saturday, 14 October, the Royal Family were reported to have breakfasted before seven, and two hours later Prince Albert drove to the new premises of the Literary and Philosophical Society in Albion Street (henceforth the Royal Institution).

Soon after his return he joined the Queen and children on the balcony of the hotel for the most memorable part of the programme. A vast amphitheatre had been erected to accommodate 10,552 Sunday school children, who, on a perfect autumn morning with a 'serene sky' overhead, sang the National Anthem to the little homely figure who, incredibly, was the symbol of imperial power. 'There was no heart in that vast assembly free from the deepest emotion, and Her Majesty was affected even to tears.'

A cavalcade then followed a circuitous route through the town centre until it reached the Pier, where the Queen borrowed a sword and commanded the Mayor to kneel, then rise as Sir Henry Cooper. In an imaginative grand climax the royal yacht sailed down the River Hull and through the town docks before taking the Royal Family to Grimsby, where they entrained for London.

In an orgy of loyalty the Old Dock became Queen's Dock, Junction Dock, Prince's Dock and the Station Hotel the Royal Station Hotel. Later developments have removed the 'Station' but, thankfully, it retains the 'Royal' description, earned by its hospitality to a distinguished guest.

THE COLONEL AND THE COUNCILLOR

Colonel Thomas Marten and Councillor Daniel Boyes

Beverley pedestrians who complain about footpaths will feel sympathy for a Victorian councillor who decided to take the law into his own hands. The sequel to this drastic action, however, should make them think twice before following his example.

The problem was the trees in the grounds of St. Mary's Manor overhanging the pavement in North Bar Within. Whether the principal grievance was the size of the branches or the falling leaves which created (as they still do) a dangerously slippery surface in wet weather isn't clear, but, whatever the impetus, Daniel Boyes, one of Beverley's most colourful councillors, decided in 1851 that enough was enough. Early in the morning of 26 February a band of workmen acting under his instructions lopped the trees both inside and outside the garden wall.

To say that the occupant of St. Mary's Manor, Colonel Thomas Marten, then serving with his regiment in Nottingham, was angered by this assault on his property would be an understatement. A notice had previously been served on him requiring him to trim his trees and he had written to his solicitor stating 'that he should yield in obedience to the law' if the Council had the right to issue such an order, but, if they were exceeding their authority, 'he would resist their doing so to the utmost the law would allow him'.

He had been promised that no action would be taken until 1 March 'to give him time to consider what course he would adopt', and he was understandably

St. Mary's Manor: the finest frontage looked towards the garden.

astonished when he heard that Boyes' posse of woodcutters had jumped the gun. Marten was an officer and a gentleman, a member of Beverley's Tory establishment, and not a man prepared to accept such an outrage inspired by a Liberal councillor. His military career had begun in 1813 and he had served with distinction, particularly at the Battle of Waterloo.

St. Mary's Manor had become his home after the death of his father-in-law, Henry Ellison, who had rebuilt the house in the early 19th century, and, although a military man by profession, 'he had a great fancy, amounting almost to a passion, for his garden', and the grounds were kept in excellent condition.

This assault on his beloved domain was not a matter to be borne lightly and accordingly, in July 1851, the case of *Marten v Boyes and Others* came to court. There could hardly have been opponents more contrasting both in life-style and character. Boyes had been landlord of the Valiant Soldier before taking over the Angel, and, never a shrinking violet, he brought great fame to his hostelry by providing a monster game pie for his customers each New Year's Day. More seriously, he was a power in the Liberal Party and so dominant in organising the campaigns of Liberal parliamentary candidates (and heavily involved in the bribery which was then a standard part of an election) that he earned himself the title 'Prime Minister of Beverley'.

In court Marten's counsel argued that Boyes had been less concerned about the public welfare than the fact that the trees obscured the inn sign of the King's Arms, whose landlady, Mrs. Ackrill, just happened to be related to him by marriage. Boyes' counsel in response marvelled at Colonel Marten's proceeding with such ' a trumpery case' and alleged that it would never have been brought but for party politics.

Perhaps he was right. In spite of the plea that it was all too trivial to bring before a court of law, the jury decided in favour of Marten and he was awarded a surely excessive £800 damages. In order to raise this sum, the Council was forced to levy an extra rate, not a move calculated to please the public. Nevertheless it provided the Tories with a useful rallying cry at future elections: 'Who chopped down Colonel Marten's trees?'

A MAN OF PROPERTY

Joseph Sykes

'Are there any books about Joseph Sykes?' was a recent enquiry from a correspondent in Bath, interested in learning more about an ancestor whom family historians would now describe as his 4 x great-grandfather.

The Sykes are fond of re-using the same Christian names in different generations, and the Joseph Sykes in question was a High Street merchant, a power in 18th-century Hull and the founding father of the branch of the family known as the Sykes of Westella. His father, Richard, married twice and it was the descendants of his first wife, Mary Kirby, who were the fortunate inheritors of the Sledmere estate and eventually the recipients of a baronetcy. After Mary's death Richard married Martha Donkin, and their son, Joseph, was born in 1723.

He was not, therefore, the first-born son and heir, but there was no hint of inferiority about his character or life-style. His house at 42 High Street served both as private residence and headquarters of Sykes & Co, one of the town's leading commercial concerns. At the rear

Joseph Sykes.

of the premises was the River Hull, where Joseph Sykes' ships sailed in from Sweden with cargoes of the white iron ore in which the firm held a virtual monopoly and which was in great demand in a Sheffield transformed by the Industrial Revolution. Sykes & Co prospered, and in the 12-year period from 1788 returned dividends totalling 160% of capital invested.

Never before had the town witnessed such a dazzling display of wealth and talent as it did in that golden period of prosperity. Joseph was a prominent member of Hull's merchant aristocracy and it was natural that he should consider it both his duty and right to exert his influence in civic affairs. He became an alderman, served one term as Sheriff, and was elected Mayor (there was no Lord Mayor until 1914) on two occasions, always making the expansion of the port his principal objective.

When he first joined the family firm Hull was still constrained by its medieval walls, and all shipping was confined to the river. Joseph had quickly realised the urgency of creating a dock if the port was ever to fulfil its potential, and, like many Georgian entrepreneurs, being more concerned about progress than conservation, achieved his aim when the walls were demolished and the first dock (now Queens Gardens) opened in 1778.

The profits of trade enabled him to become a major investor in property. In Hull he purchased the Mason estate and such names as Sykes Street, Mason Street and Bourne Street – Bourne was a relation by marriage – are evidence of his activities as a developer. No merchant worth his salt could be without a country estate, and, although the High Street house was an impressive mansion, fronted by iron railings, with marble steps leading to its entrance, and coach house and stabling opposite, in 1756 he became a country gentleman when he bought Westella Hall, enlarging the house, improving the grounds, and, like later members of his family, enhancing the appearance of Kirkella and Westella.

Joseph was the father of six sons and one daughter and, contrary to a common occurrence, his talent and abilities were passed on to the next generation. Two sons, John and Nicholas (from whom my Bath correspondent is descended), followed in his footsteps as Mayor and Sheriff, but the fifth son, Daniel, of Raywell, was to earn greater fame as M. P. for Hull and later for Beverley. The marriage of the only daughter, Marianne, however, eventually led to a descendant of international status: the author, E. M. Forster, was Joseph's great-great-grandson.

There are references to Joseph Sykes in many publications, but, as far as I know, no complete biography. He certainly deserves one as a man whose impact on the area was immense and whose influence did not end with his death.

HESSLE SPICE CAKE AND HULL CHEESE

Local food and drink

Local dishes and drinks have taken a heavy battering from supermarkets, which make produce from all over the country – indeed, all over the world – available anywhere and almost at any season. All very different from the time when each town, village and even family had its own jealously guarded recipes.

This threat to regional differences, though, has made some cookery writers all the more concerned to ensure that traditional foods do not pass into history. East Yorkshire tends not to feature as prominently as other parts of the county in their writing, though one excellent book, *A Taste of Yorkshire*, by Theodora Fitzgibbon, includes some local dishes, all new to me. Hessle Spice Cake is one (Hessle is well known for its spice cake, the author claims) and there is also Wansford Steak, though this appears to be a hotel speciality rather than a traditional dish. Another book, *Old Yorkshire Recipes* by Joan Poulson, has Beverley Spiced Beef, a reminder of the value placed on spices in pre-refrigeration days. Hull, after all, has its Land of Green Ginger, one of the most famous street names in England and the one raising the most controversy.

Brandy snap may not be unique to this area but it is the traditional delicacy of Hull Fair. Theodora Fitzgibbon elevates its historical status when she describes it, along with waffles, as one of the last surviving relics of medieval wafers. Surely, too, we should give Hull credit for being a pioneer of a dish which is now universally regarded as traditionally English as roast beef but which has its origin only in the 19th century: fish and chips.

Much rarer, and a real local delicacy, is rock semper (or samphire), a fleshy green plant with a stringy stem, sometimes known as 'poor man's asparagus', which is collected on the South Holderness coast and either eaten as a cooked vegetable or pickled and served with cold meat.

Yorkshire, not just the East Riding, will forever be associated with Yorkshire Pudding, though some pubs and restaurants now concentrate on size more than quality – connoisseurs expect a proper Yorkshire Pudding to melt in the mouth. Some people still serve it in the traditional way, as a starter, a lingering legacy from an agricultural past when farm workers were given their pudding before their main course so that hearty appetites would be dulled, and were wickedly urged to eat more: 'Whoever eats most pudding gets most meat!'

Yorkshire curd cheesecakes (pronounced 'crud chisseks' in the countryside) are still sufficiently local for a lecturer who recently visited Beverley to ask for advice on finding the shop which sold the best so that he could return to London with evidence of his travels in the far North. The genuine ones, he was told, have a gooey base where the moisture is beginning to seep into the pastry. South Cave, apparently, is a local centre of excellence where curd cheesecakes are made to authentic recipes.

Shrove Tuesday pancakes are another surviving tradition, though most of the local customs of the day are long since gone: like the ringing of the 'Pancake Bell' from Hedon Church by apprentices nearing the end of their indentures as a signal for residents to get out their frying pans. Hedon, however, still has its punch made to a secret recipe and served by the Mayor on special occasions, a mixture so potent that Georgian and Victorian aldermen who drank too deeply had to be transported home in a wheelbarrow manpowered by the Sergeant at Mace.

But no one could beat Hull's reputation for strong ale, the most powerful brew of all being 'Hull Cheese', which contained more than the usual quantity of solid matter, the result, according to experts, of poor filtering. 'Hull', wrote the 19th-century historian, Sheahan, 'was formerly as famous for good ale as Burton upon Trent is at the present day,' and he quoted an advertisement to attract volunteers to the local militia which offered as a perk the advantage of being quartered in a town where excellent ale was sold at only three-pence a quart, best quality fish at a penny a pound, and meat in the Shambles was cheaper than at any other place in the Kingdom. A Heaven upon Earth!

CHRISTMAS DAY IN THE WORKHOUSE
Christmas, 1910

A Christmas Carol, Dickens' famous novel, has a close rival in the nostalgia stakes – the *Hull Daily Mail* in the years before the First World War. Christmas then was enjoyed all the more intensely because it began later and provided an all too brief period of perfect happiness in what was for many a life of limited pleasures. Decades later, the columns of the local press of the time still have the power to revive a breath of the heady atmosphere of those Christmases long past.

Take 1910, for example, when a lengthy article,

SCULCOATES WORKHOUSE.

"I am sorry we are going to lose the Master, but may God bless him and the whole of the family. May God speed them and look after them wherever they go." In a voice of emotion an old inmate, Douglas Garton, stood up at the end of the concert at the Sculcoates Workhouse on Monday night, and voiced the sentiments of all the old men and women. "Amen," muttered an old man near by, and several old people wiped their eyes. Then another old man, who is known as Cobbler Bob, rose and remarked, "We are all very sorry he has had the trouble he has had, and is going to leave us."

Guardian Eastman, the fairy godfather of the proceedings, who had arranged the concert, and kept everyone merry with his breezy comments, said that there had been the shadow of the death of the Matron, whose memory they cherished, and now there was another shadow in the forthcoming retirement of the Master, which was a source of regret to every inmate and member of the Board. He hoped that time would eventually heal the wounds, and in God's good time all suffering would be over, and when they had done with their merry Christmases on earth they would go to that place where He who was born on Christmas Day had gone to prepare a place for them.

The Master, who spoke with some emotion, gladly thanked the artistes at the request of the chairman. He felt that he could hardly do so, for Mr Eastman had made a reference to a matter very dear to his heart. This was the last occasion (Boxing night) on which he should be able to move such a vote. Year after year he had always assisted in these concerts, and he had done his best to make them a success in days gone by. The Master explained that the old folk why the Mayor and Sheriff had not attended the previous day's dinner.

The concert was just the kind for a Christmas party, and Mr Eastman, who was in a most jovial mood, repeatedly asked the gathering to declare "whether things were going all right." He was even so accommodating as to deliberately put back the clock above the platform two hours, and calling up William King, the foreman joiner, jokingly reprimanded him for not having kept his word and stopped the clock. "I told him to do so," declared an old man in a thin voice at the back of the large dining hall. There proved to be a plentiful supply of artistes who provided a splendidly varied concert. Mr Seth King, comedian, was a host in himself, and Mr Charles McLean, who renewed his acquaintance with the audience after ten years absence, was a great favourite. He sang and danced in the style of a first-class professional, and showed his

From the Hull Daily Mail *(Christmas 1910).*

'Christmas at the Shops', contained masses of detail which the passage of time has turned into romance. At Bladon's in Prospect Street 'a Renaissance lace night dress case 'was a tempting bargain at 2/11d, while 'the designs and patterns in fancy handkerchiefs' were by far the best the store had ever offered, with prices as low as 2¾d making them 'useful and inexpensive presents'. Mr. Goulden, 'the enterprising King Edward Street gentlemen's outfitter', offered 'warm, smart dressing gowns' at prices ranging from 21/- to 27/6d, and Manfield & Son of Whitefriargate were selling dress shoes and slippers for ladies and gentlemen in designs which were 'refined, exclusive and correct'.

The weather that December was unusually mild, and many butchers had waited in vain for frost before slaughtering their stock. In the Market Hall, however, Messrs. Smith and Bell had put on fine displays, and Mr. J. W. Gould was showing his heavy beast, Jolly Jumbo, fated to have no chance of being around for the Christmas fun.

Shops remained open late on Christmas Eve and some people even posted their cards in the evening, confident they would be delivered next morning. Hectic last-minute trade made the town centre a succession of 'animated scenes', and in the main shopping streets 'it was difficult to make much progress'.

In 1910 Christmas Day fell on a Sunday, and, in an age when religious observances were more strictly kept, many preferred to delay the secular celebrations until the Monday. Yet nothing dimmed the sheer delight of the Day itself: 'Christmas bells rang out from the church towers, peals of hope and joy; sunshine flooded the street, the air was crisp and thousands of people were happy.'

Some of the happiest were the crowds of children, many shoeless and stockingless, who skipped along the streets, 'hungry, ill-clothed, ill-cared for, probably, but still apparently light-hearted', on their way to the Assembly Rooms or one of the other places where a free meal was provided for the needy.

At the Anlaby Road Workhouse the 'usual discipline' was relaxed on Christmas Day. but the real festivities began on Boxing Day, with a breakfast of bread and butter and tea, followed by a dinner of roast beef and plum pudding. The Sculcoates Workhouse inmates were treated to a concert by 'a plentiful supply of artistes', among them Mr. Charles McLean, who 'showed his versatility by a solo on the bones' and an elocutionist who 'kept the audience laughing heartily with wholesome fun'.

A religious service preceded dinner at the Newland Orphan Homes, and 'conspicuous here was the great three-tiered Christmas cake sent by Sir James and Lady Reckitt'. There was vociferous cheering when the civic party entered, and the Mayor told the children that 'their happy condition brought back to his mind the 1,200 poor and ill-kept children he had just left', with such effect that 'sympathy for their less fortunate fellows was evidenced in the faces of the children'.

Reminding orphans of their luck may not be the most tactful Christmas message, but perhaps people were less cynical in 1910. What could be more innocent than the excitement in the Prince's Hall cinema, where an audience of anxious 'little folk', always on the side of right, 'cheered mightily as they watched a woman climb over a cliff to stop two men fighting, and shouted encouragement to make her move more quickly? It was an innocence soon to be shattered by the horrors of the real world.

THE MAKING OF A MASTERPIECE

Winifred Holtby's South Riding

The East Riding regained its rightful place of honour in the last round of local government reforms, but more famous than any of Yorkshire's three Ridings is the one which exists only in fiction, the 'South Riding', given literary immortality by Winifred Holtby's famous novel published in 1936.

The South Riding she created is based on the part of East Yorkshire which she knew intimately, though most of the story is set in Holderness: rather remarkably, as it was an area she came to know well only in the last two years of her short life. She was born in 1898 in Rudston, and to her the Wolds would always be a microcosm of the English countryside at its best. 'Half my life and all my mind are bound up with it,' she wrote after her career as a journalist had taken her to London and abroad. Her friend, Vera Brittain, also believed that to the end of Winifred's days the view from her bedroom window at the rear of Rudston House dominated her memory 'and throughout her youth it made a permanent background to her stories and dreams'.

A strike of agricultural workers in 1918 so depressed her father, David, that he gave up his substantial farm and retired to Cottingham, a move which Winifred felt as exile from the natural spaciousness of the Wolds to the bourgeois constraints of suburbia. But a novelist can turn the unhappiest experiences into books which give pleasure. Rudston was transformed into the fictional 'Anderby' and, although it did not feature prominently in *South Riding*, the farmworkers' strike provided the plot for an earlier novel, *Anderby Wold*.

Cottingham could never match Rudston, but Winifred was not blind to its beauty. 'Tonight even Cottingham looked lovely as I

Winifred Holtby's map of her fictional South Riding (from the Winifred Holtby Guide: *Winifred Holtby Committee 1983).*

46

came down from the station about five o'clock and heard the winter birds,' she told Vera in 1926. As 'Marshington', it formed the background for another novel, *The Crowded Street*, and, more significantly, played a fundamental part in the evolution of *South Riding*. Cottingham was on the line to Beverley, and Winifred's mother, Alice, became an enthusiastic member of the East Riding County Council and its first woman alderman. With great imagination Winifred used Mrs. Holtby's dull committee papers to orchestrate a drama of memorable characters whose lives were affected by the decisions of the South Riding County Council, with headquarters in 'Flintonbridge' a close replica of County Hall in Beverley.

Cottingham was convenient for Hull, a city which Winifred described as having 'character' and for which she coined the perfect fictional name of 'Kingsport'. Hull gave her the title for another novel, *Land of Green Ginger*, in which Whitefriargate appears as 'Friarsgate'. In the Central Library in Albion Street ('Willoughby Place') she studied back copies of the *Hull Daily Mail*, noting details of local events and personalities which she could weave into the plot of *South Riding*. The book was an instant success – with everyone except Alderman Mrs. Holtby, who was horrified that so many of its incidents and characters could be identified with their originals.

Increasing ill-health took Winifred to Holderness, an unspectacular area but with a distinctive atmosphere to which she was acutely sensitive. In 1934 she rented a cottage in Withernsea ('Kiplington'), where she could recuperate, but all the time she was busily absorbing impressions of the town and its people. Though *South Riding* was still unwritten, it existed in embryo and only time was needed to bring it to fruition. 'One day I must write about Withernsea, the town everybody wants to leave,' she had decided.

Much of the writing was done the following year in Hornsea, where she had rented rooms, and it was now that she found the elegiac words to describe this lonely region with 'great ships gliding up to Kingsport, seen from low-lying windows as though they moved across the fields'.

The Wolds were her first love, but Holderness came a close second.

Winifred Holtby.

THE MOVING STORY OF WILLIAM WILBERFORCE

Wilberforce Monument

William Wilberforce's statue on its massive column at the eastern end of Queens Gardens manages to remain a dominant feature of the City's skyline in spite of competition from high-rise buildings of more recent years. Its air of permanence, however, is deceptive. Since it was erected over a century and a half ago it has undergone a moving experience remarkable even for Hull, which has a habit of uprooting statues and fixing them in new locations.

From the first there was doubt about the best place for a memorial to the Hull-born statesman who had died in London on 29 July 1833. He was buried in Westminster Abbey, and there was a strong surge of feeling that he should also be honoured in his home town. A public meeting was held on 12 August and it was resolved that 'an obelisk or pillar will form the most striking and appropriate memorial'.

John Clark, a Leeds architect, who was commissioned to supervise the project, suggested a number of possible locations, one a site at the southern end of Queen Street, near the pier, and another a central position in Kingston Square. But the place finally selected was the one he least favoured: near the junction of two town docks at what was to become known as Monument Bridge.

Hull people always knew how to celebrate in style and, very appropriately, the laying of the foundation stone on 1 August 1834 coincided with the day when all slaves in the British colonies at long last became free. Crowds gathered to witness this historic occasion. Shops were shut, flags flew from ships, bells rang from the churches and spectators occupied every conceivable place with a view, even the roof and tower of St. John's Church (now replaced by the Ferens Art Gallery). For some strange reason the Mayor refused to attend, and

Wilberforce Monument at its present location, where it was moved in 1935: its one and only move.

consequently the man who wielded the silver trowel and paid an eloquent tribute to Wilberforce was Richard Bethell, one of the M.P.s for Yorkshire, as Wilberforce had been before him.

A local firm of builders, Myers and Wilson, was employed to raise the 'elegant, fluted Doric column' and by April 1835 two-thirds of its 90-foot height had been completed. Only then was it decided to surmount the column with a statue showing Wilberforce 'in his senatorial robes with a folded scroll in his right hand'. All was finished by the second week in November.

A century elapsed before the next chapter in the story. By the 1930s Hull was trying to cope with an ever-increasing amount of motorised transport and Wilberforce Column and Monument Bridge were a nuisance to traffic. Queens Dock was too far inland and too small for modern shipping and, in a radical scheme, it was decided to fill it in, get rid of the Bridge and at the same time move Wilberforce, a feat which some thought impossible but which the prominent builder and councillor, R. G. Tarran, offered to undertake at his own expense.

'Wilberforce is down!' reported the *Hull Times* on Saturday, 20 April 1935. On the previous Tuesday Queen Victoria Square had been like a football ground 'with an important cup-tie going on in the air'. It was raining and windy, but, once again, spectators occupied every vantage point. St. John's Church had gone but now the Dock Office roof and the balcony of the City Hall gave grandstand views.

'A comparatively easy job,' Councillor Tarran had previously commented. Just before noon he climbed the windlashed ladders to the top of the monument, and then descended to give the order to begin. A crane slowly raised its head, and one of the workmen shouted, 'She's going down grand, boys!', as 'Wilberforce slid from his ancient base, still wearing that inscrutable smile.'

He was re-erected where he stands today, and the persistent myth that he was moved a second time has – unlike the column – no foundation whatever.

THE CITY'S PERFECT ENGLISH VILLAGE

The Garden Village

The Garden Village is a name which sets one's imagination going with pictures of an idyllic English countryside. And, in spite of modern developments all around, the winding tree-lined roads of Hull's Garden Village and its attractive houses still retain something of the atmosphere of the Edwardian area when a vision became a reality.

The man with the vision was the philanthropic industrialist, Sir James Reckitt, who in 1907 put his ideas to his colleague, T. R. Ferens: 'Whilst I and my family are living in beautiful houses, surrounded by fine gardens and lovely scenery, the work people we employ are, many of them, living in squalor'. His solution was to establish a Garden Village within reasonable distance of the factory so that those who wanted could have a better house

with a garden for the same rent they were already paying for inferior accommodation, 'and with the advantage of fresher air and such clubs and outdoor amusements as are usually found in rural surroundings'.

The Garden Village.

This was not the first scheme of its kind. Sir James had probably been influenced by the creation of Cadbury's Bournville, and the Hull project benefited from such earlier examples. The plan was co-ordinated by the local firm of architects, Runton and Barry, and the result was their total supervision of every aspect of the work and a guarantee that everything was of the highest quality.

The selected site was part of the estate of B. M. Jalland of Holderness House, a mansion originally so rural that even in the 1860s it was described as a residence 'in the immediate vicinity of Hull', with a fine elm-lined avenue which had once been 'an ancient cart road which led from the high road to some farms'. Even after the disposal of the estate it remained a house of distinction and in 1909 became the home of T. R. Ferens.

The official opening of the Garden Village took place on 1 July 1908. It was a lovely summer's day and a large audience sat or stood around as Sir James spoke from the balcony of a house on a characteristic theme: the need for people of wealth to use their money and energy 'for the betterment of those about them'. Formalities over, everyone adjourned to two large marquees for tea, and many took the opportunity to inspect one or two of the houses still unoccupied.

Although the scheme was in its early days, they should have been impressed. Instead of monotonous rows of terraced housing, all of uniform size and appearance, there was the variety of style and layout characteristic of a real village but created here in a design which showed considerable artistry and imagination. The result was a most effective townscape with a wide spread of houses which looked like homes, no more than an average of 12 to an acre, and in a range of sizes and rents to suit the differing needs of tenants.

It was, above all, intended to be a community. There was a village green, or oval, as a central feature, a village hall (since demolished), and a village club. No pub, of course, for both Reckitt and Ferens frowned on drinking, and the question was asked to which only one answer was expected: 'What man is there who is not physically and morally improved by taking an interest in gardening and horticulture?'

A local poet, inspired to poke a little gentle fun at the lofty aims of the enterprise, pretended to envy those who benefited from such munificence:

'Garden Village folk are glad,
And filled with laughter blithe and gay,
Whose country house is in the town,
Finds life a glorious holiday.'

Since those halcyon days before the First World War a different world has come into existence, and change has affected the Garden Village. The architects never envisaged a nation of car owners, but the gardens they provided have proved big enough for garages.

WILD MEN OF THE WESTWOOD
A Beverley Riot, 1861

Beverley Westwood should be a peaceful place: over 600 acres of grassland fringed by Burton Bushes, a remnant of the great forest which once covered the entire area, and with a distant view of the town which grew up in the hollow down below.

Yet its history has been remarkably turbulent. In the Middle Ages it was the subject of intense dispute between the Archbishops of York, who wanted to keep it as a private hunting ground, and the people of Beverley, who regarded it as theirs by 'ancient right'. The Westwood was a valuable asset for residents of a country town, providing wood for building, clay for brick-making, chalk for making roads and for processing in lime-kilns, and, of course, pasturage for their animals.

Not until 1380 was the long-running issue settled when Archbishop Neville agreed that for an annual rent of 100 shillings p.a. the Westwood would remain under the control of the townsmen for ever. Even so, there were many later incidents which disturbed the rural peace. The Westwood was an obvious venue for meetings and demonstrations, and in 1536 it was the rallying place for rebels who joined the Pilgrimage of Grace in an attempt to oppose the religious changes of Henry VIII. Such unpleasant recreations as bull-baiting lingered there after it was banned in the town, and some of the sports where humans battled against each other were more noted for their violence than their sophisticated tactics.

But an insurrection in 1861 aroused more local interest than anything in its past history. The problem was that Archbishop Neville's grant had been made to a Beverley where freemen alone had the right to vote. In 1835, however, a much needed reform brought ratepayers on to the electoral roll, and the newly elected Council could not have the same rights over the Westwood as its predecessor. The result was a private Act of Parliament placing the pasturage of the Westwood under the control of Pasture Masters elected by the freemen, but allowing the Council to retain the soil, and so the freehold.

It was a complicated arrangement likely to lead to future problems, and a tricky situation occurred in 1861 when a long lease granted by the old Council came to an end. It related to a piece of land on the edge of the Westwood, Butt Close, on which the Fishwick family had a mill and which they now demolished in accordance with the terms of the agreement.

This was the moment for the freemen to strike. Butt Close, they claimed, was originally part of the Westwood and now reverted to them, not to the Council. On 2 September tension mounted as the bellman, John Duffill, announced a meeting of freemen to be held that evening on 'their bit of ground'. The fun in store was too good even for non-freemen to miss and ' a large concourse' of Beverlonians of all ages and types assembled. So did the police, but, when Sergeant Dunn tried to prevent Duffill entering the forbidden territory, Duffill took a running jump and surmounted a gate Dunn was defending. Hordes followed their leader and the police decided that discretion was the better part of valour and withdrew, though not before taking the names of the leading miscreants.

Duffill ascended the mound on which the mill had stood and addressed his troops, who sat proudly in tiered ranks, some of them smoking their 'pipes of victory'. Those who preferred to see a bit more action then decided to demolish the house where the

Fishwick's Mill.

Fishwicks had lived and completed the job by setting it on fire.

Beverley Council was not prepared to accept such a humiliating defeat and retribution came in October when 40 men were brought to court, but, although six were fined modest amounts, the charges against the rest were dropped. Some of the freemen regretted that their victory had been gained too easily, and, deprived of a vigorous court-room battle, assembled in Saturday Market to enjoy a rousing speech from their counsel, whose services were, sadly, no longer needed.

It makes the current controversy about female freemen sound very tame.

FEASTS OF FUN

Friendly Societies

A feast is a very special event, and it is only right that it was used to describe the celebrations which were once the high points in the social calendar of many East Riding villages.

Grandest of all were probably the summer feasts of friendly societies, those self-help organisations in which working men pooled their modest contributions to provide basic welfare benefits long before the State system came into being. June was a popular time for these colourful occasions which aroused enormous local interest, even from non-members and particularly from children, glad of an excuse for missing school.

On 3 June 1898 a number of club feasts fortunately coincided with exceptionally fine weather. At Lund the day followed the traditional pattern described by Dr. David Neave in his publication, *Feasts, Fellowship and Financial Aid*, with a lodge meeting of Oddfellows at 9 a.m. before a procession, led by the Nafferton Saxhorn Brass Band, to the church for an edifying sermon by a visiting preacher. Serious business over, the Oddfellows paraded again through the village 'which presented a very gay appearance, the day being observed as a general holiday'. At the Wellington Inn 100 sat down to a dinner 'served by Host Turner in his usual good style' and, not surprisingly after the morning's activities, 'did full justice to the viands'. Then came one of those orgies of oratory in which Victorians took such delight and at which toasts alternated with music. The village green was covered

An outing from the Ebenezer Chapel, Spring Bank, Hull.

with stalls, and in the evening of this day to remember many visitors arrived to join in the fun.

Nearby, at Middleton, the Ancient Order of Foresters celebrated in similar fashion, with a procession in full regalia and a sumptuous dinner in a marquee in a field near the Robin Hood. The day, though, had a more military flavour. Music was provided by the Driffield Volunteers and the sermon was on the text, 'Quit yourselves like men and fight'. In his after-dinner speech the preacher toasted the army, navy and reserve forces, while other speakers complained of the low number of recruits from the East Riding and urged more young men to join the army.

The Leconfield Oddfellows also sat down to dinner in a marquee but, living in one of those rare villages without a pub, had their meal provided by the landlord of the Duke of Wellington, then near Lockington Station. Speakers there concentrated on the remarkable progress made by a lodge which, starting 88 years before with 12 members and no capital, had secured over 170 members and substantial assets of £2,329.

Feasts were not the monopoly of friendly societies. Well into this century there were memorable Sunday School Feasts where the highlights were usually a procession, a church or chapel service, and a magnificent Yorkshire tea. Villages such as Preston had enough organisations to offer a round of summer entertainment, with the Wesleyan Sunday School Treat, the Church School Feast, the Druids' Feast and the Primitive Methodist Outing. For children such outings were a long-awaited opportunity to venture outside home territory. In the years before the First World War two or three wagons or rullies with seats for passengers and drawn by horses, resplendent in brasses and ribbons, would leave Thorngumbald at 7 am en route to Withernsea. The ride was slow, and it was nearly midday before they arrived, but the sheer delight of a few hours at the seaside made it all worthwhile.

A breath of fresh air was even more valued by city children. In August 1911 the Central Hull annual poor children's outing was to Beverley Westwood. Horses and rullies were lent by B.O.C.M. and Mr. J. Smith of Lime Street, and 200 children enjoyed a meal of ham, bread and butter, spice bread and tea.

To anyone who survived on plain fare the rest of the year this was nothing short of a feast.

A DICKENS OF A VISIT

Charles Dickens in Hull

Book-signing sessions and literary luncheons are popular occasions for bringing together authors and their admiring readers, but no modern writer has ever had the impact Charles Dickens achieved by his personal appearances. All he did was stand alone on a stage and read from his works, but these were readings with a difference. As he read, he was a man transformed who seemed to become the characters born in his imagination, and his audiences were in raptures of laughter or tears as they saw them re-created before their very eyes.

He was in Hull in the autumn of 1858, the year in which he started the series of tours which were to take him all over the country as well as to Ireland and the United States. His Hull visit was the triumphant success regularly repeated wherever he appeared over the next 12 years.

The venue was the Assembly Rooms, Jarratt Street (now the New Theatre), and he began by telling his audience that they were 'not to restrain their feelings during the reading – to applaud when they feel pleased'. They took him at his word, and, as he read one of their favourite books, *A Christmas Carol*, they felt that for the first time they had 'caught its meaning'.

Some of his friends thought he was demeaning his status as a great writer by these public performances, but writing is a solitary occupation, he was a born actor who loved applause, and the readings were extremely profitable. Although his writing brought him a substantial income, he had three households to support, his own, his estranged wife's, and, unknown to most of his readers, the discreet establishment of his mistress, Ellen Ternan, actress daughter of a Hull-born actress.

He was back in Hull in 1859, but then came a ten-year interval before he returned in March 1869. On that occasion an incident occurred which was only publicly revealed in the *Hull Daily Mail* in 1927 when a Mr. Edward Simpson Long died. As a young man in his mid-twenties he had worked as an assistant to Henry Dixon of 28 Whitefriargate, a dealer in fancy goods.

During his visit of 1869 Dickens called in at the shop to buy ladies' stockings and, unrecognised, started a friendly conversation with young Mr. Long, who explained that he could not go the reading that night as it was only for subscribers. Dickens then rather naughtily asked if he had read any of Dickens' books. Fortunately Long was able to reply that he had, and he was then asked which he preferred. Before he left the shop Dickens handed him his card on which he had written, 'Please Admit Bearer'. He departed, and Long was naturally astounded to realise that he had been talking to the great man himself.

The evening was another roaring success and Long was given a seat on the platform close to Dickens' reading desk. Included in the programme were extracts from *Pickwick Papers* and 'a most thrilling episode from *Oliver Twist*'. Once again Dickens proved himself excellent at comedy and tragedy alike. During his readings he kept turning round to see how Long was enjoying himself and it was clear that he had chosen passages from all his favourite books.

For Mr. Long this was a memorable encounter. He was, of course, completely unaware of the existence of Ellen Ternan and one thing always puzzled him: why the distinguished elderly author should be buying ladies' silk stockings.

Charles Dickens: advertisement for a reading.

THOSE OTHER BEVERLEYS

Beverley, Australia

Beverley is such an attractive name that it's hardly surprising to find it duplicated in other parts of the world. One of these Beverleys, in Western Australia, owes its origin to a young man born in the Yorkshire Beverley.

Charles Simmons was the first colonial surgeon appointed to serve in that part of Australia, and obviously a man of some ability to have risen from a modest background. He was baptised on 18 February 1802 in St. Mary's Church, the son of George Simmons, a breeches maker who had been described as a glover when he married Sarah Andrews at Foston on the Wolds in 1783. George and Sarah settled in Beverley, and Charles was their fifth child born in the town.

How Charles managed to make the leap from tradesman's son to surgeon is unknown, but at the age of 26, with the initials 'M.D.' after his name, he left England in January 1829 on the *Parmelia*, Australia-bound. It was a hazardous and eventful journey, with his assistant surgeon drowning in an accident at Cape Town, but finally, on 3 June, he was landed on a wet and windswept beach at Garden Island.

Few preparations had been made for the arrival of the settlers and one writer has commented that, if Simmons had been older and better established in his profession, he would never have been tempted to try his luck in 'a raw new colony on the other side of the world'. His payment of 15 shillings per day (defined in that way as a reminder that he was expected to work seven days a week) did, however, bring him an annual salary of £273 and made him one of the highest paid colonial officials. He was the only bachelor among them, and a fellow passenger remarked that his broad Yorkshire accent made him appear 'rather strange', though, he admitted, Simmons could still 'prove a clever man'.

Medical conditions were primitive in East Yorkshire, but far worse in Australia. After Simmons managed to get his stores and equipment ashore, a hut had to serve both as home and surgery, but his spirits remained high. 'During the month of June,' he wrote, 'I have not had any sick owing to the peculiar healthiness of the climate.' This happy state of affairs was not to last. In the autumn he moved to Perth and found scurvy a great problem among soldiers stationed there.

He was also sent to various places to report on their suitability for settlers and was given land for himself in the vicinity of Beverley, so named in honour of the town of his birth. Charles Simmons had left his mark on Australia but his own period there was brief. He was suddenly taken ill and died in October 1831, still in his twenties. His grave in East Perth Cemetery is unmarked.

I am most grateful to Mr. Peter Calvert of Molescroft (well known for his talk on the Brandesburton pygmies) for drawing my attention to the career of this young Beverley man who has not so far received his fair share of fame. Tourist material which Mr. Calvert has lent me shows that the Beverley of Western Australia (described as an 'undiscovered jewel' where you can enjoy the 'uncluttered charm' of old colonial days) has a St. Mary's Church, and places named York and Seaton Ross Hill are not far away.

There's another Beverley in South Australia, founded by E.N. Emmett, who is understood to have come from our own Beverley, and a Beverly without the 'e' in the United States, as well as the famous Beverly Hills. Most intriguing of all, though, is a small town in France called St. Jean de Brevelay with relics in the church which reputedly are those of St. John of Beverley. How they ended up there is likely to remain a mystery.

DIRECTIONS TO THE PAST

Directories

'Where do you start?' people often ask when they first become interested in research into local or family history.

There's no point in re-discovering what already exists in print, and a popular starting point is often one of the directories published (at irregular intervals) from the 18th century onwards. It may sound odd to find directories before the age of the telephone, but, with growing trade, there was a need for a practical reference book which would quickly give the kind of information a businessman might require. These directories, it is important to remember, were prepared for everyday use, not for future historians, and the early ones are, regrettably, very selective in the names of residents they include.

The Hull directory of 1791 was quite a slim volume but it's a fascinating one to browse through, and more effective in bringing the Georgian town vividly to life than many academic tomes. Original copies of old directories are now collectors' items but a reprint of this one in the excellent Malet Lambert Local History series has made it easily accessible at a modest price.

Some famous names stand out from the ranks of their less distinguished contemporaries, though in that period when an 's' was printed as 'f', even familiar names can look strange. There is Dr. John Alderson M.D. of Savile Street, Dockside, and Richard Baker, snuff and tobacco manufacturer of Posterngate, but now remembered as a property developer who gave his name to Baker Street. Others who immediately catch the eye are Benjamin Blaydes, shipbuilder of 'Trippet, Dock Bridge', and members of the Broadley, Maister and Sykes families, major contributors to the spectacular expansion of the port.

As well as the alphabetical lists, there's a wealth of information on civic and business matters, headed by the Mayor and Aldermen, and with officers from Sheriff down to the Gaoler and Constables, all with addresses for easy contact. Probably of more immediate use, though, in a period when transport by water was often quicker than by land were the lists of vessels and details of their sailings to other places in Britain. Coach

The Criterion cinema.

services were included, and a modern reader must sigh with relief at being spared the horror of a trip to London which involved crossing the Humber and taking the coach from Barton to Lincoln the first day, proceeding to Sleaford the next, and reaching the Spread Eagle in Gracechurch Street, London, on the third, at a fare of £2. 2s. inside or £1. 4s. outside.

Even for those with no specific research in mind, town directories are marvellous for mentally wandering down familiar streets and noting the endless changes they have undergone over the years. The 1900 Hull directory lists George Street with a grocer's shop at the Grimston Street corner on the north side, and, further down, the Grand Theatre. By 1910 three well-known firms were now on the north side: R.P. Carmichael and Co, watchmakers, John Scarborough, 'phonograph exchange', and Swallow and Barry, hairdressers. Turn to the 1920 directory and, instead of the grocer's shop, there is the Majestic Picture House, and, across the road the Prince's Hall, opened in 1910 but probably too late for inclusion in the directory of that year. Later directories would show a further chapter in the story: in 1935 the Majestic became the Criterion and the Grand the Dorchester.

Both local landmarks have now disappeared, but throughout these years one institution remained

unchanged; Hull Saving Bank on its prominent corner site at the end of George Street was a symbol of continuity.

Reprinted by Malet Lambert Local History Reprints.

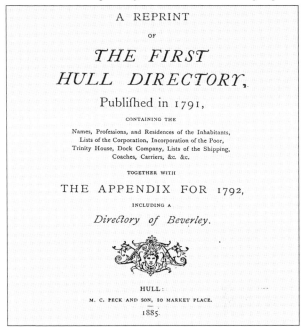

CHARITY PROVIDES A HOME

Northumberland Avenue almshouses

Do you recognise this building? It was described in an old guide book as 'one of the most pleasing and picturesque' in Hull, and in a more recent one as 'a surprising building to find in this setting', with its 'half-timbered gables and pretty corner turrets', a Tudor arched gateway and 'a great tower of unexpected and welcome fancifulness'.

Anyone who can't immediately visualise this romantic-sounding edifice need not be embarrassed, as it is off the beaten track, isolated in an industrial area. The answer is the Municipal Hospitals, or almshouses, in Northumberland Avenue; the first description comes from Brown's *Illustrated Guide* of 1891, the second from David Neave's excellent new edition of Pevsner's Guide to local buildings.

Although I must have passed it many times, it was

only last week that I had an opportunity to stop and stare both inside and out, at the kind invitation of architect Ian Rogerson, one of the 20 members of the Board of Trustees of the United Charities of Kingston upon Hull who are responsible for the impressive complex, designated as a listed building.

'Charity' and 'alms' are words now suspected because they carry a suggestion of patronising do-gooding, but before the birth of the welfare state there was a general understanding that the better-off had a moral duty to help the less fortunate, and over the centuries Hull acquired a whole range of charities, funded at different times by different individuals with specific aims in mind.

William Gee, for example, financed a hospital in Chapel Lane in 1595, while Sir John Lister's will of 1640 provided funds and premises for a hospital in South Church Side, and in 1661, during his year as mayor, High Street merchant George Crowle established a hospital in Sewer Lane. 'Hospital' then had the meaning of 'hospice' or place of refuge, not an infirmary in the modern sense.

The story of Hull's charities is quite a saga. By the 19th century there were many complaints about mismanagement by a Corporation consisting of aldermen elected for life, and in 1836, when the Corporation was reformed, control passed to Hull Charity Trustees. Some problems persisted and in 1887 the various minor hospitals in the town were amalgamated and the fine new building erected in Northumberland Avenue to the design of the eminent local architects, Smith and Brodrick, at a cost of £15,000.

Ian showed me the Board Room, which has contents guaranteed to send the adrenalin flowing through the veins of any local historian. There are framed sketches of the old hospitals which have disappeared (though some original wall plaques were rescued and incorporated in the Victorian building). One wall of the room is covered with a board honouring those who have been trustees since 1836, among them such famous names as Sir Henry Cooper, Sir Alfred Gelder and David Lister. Not so well known is Neiles Billany, in 1885 the first working man in Hull to stand for Parliament.

The original cost of the Victorian building is dwarfed by the £1½ millions spent in recent times on refurbishment, with another £100,000 going on improvement of the grounds. When the premises were opened in 1887 there were rooms for well over 100 persons. Now there are self-catering flats for 56 tenants, though 25 are at present vacant. Considerable care has been taken to reduce the institutional atmosphere which hangs over many large buildings, and the former chapel now serves as a common room where the residents can meet socially. Altogether a remarkable example of an old organisation surviving through sensible adaptation to changing needs.

Northumberland Avenue almshouses.

THINGS THAT CAUSE BUMPS IN THE FIELDS

Skipsea Castle

Hedon people were up in arms when a book published some years ago claimed that nothing now remained of the once thriving port apart from a few humps in a field. Fortunately the town has far more reminders of its medieval prosperity than the uneven ground in Far Bank, the site of a former dock, which the author probably had in mind and which was more distinctive before the filling in of the deep, grassy hollow.

But in an area as flat as ours, even humps and bumps in fields are often valuable pointers to the past and there is a wide range of possible origins. The ups and downs of Beverley Westwood sometimes show where clay or chalk was extracted and sometimes indicate prehistoric or Romano-British burial sites. Swine has its Giant's Hill which may have been nothing more than a vantage point for hunters and fowlers surveying the marshy land around, but particularly interesting are the mottes (mounds) of moated manor houses and castles. Driffield has its Moot Hill and Cottingham its Baynard's Castle, but most spectacular of all is Skipsea Castle near the Holderness coast.

Now under the control of English Heritage and invitingly advertised as, 'Open any reasonable time. Entry Free', it apparently attracts some visitors who are disappointed not to find a ruined stone castle. Most, however, would surely agree with historian Dr. Keith Allison that 'seen across the waterlogged fields through the mists of a winter's day the motte at Skipsea still makes a lasting impression'.

This formidable earthwork, 36 feet high and 328 feet in diameter at the base, with an 8-acre bailey, was built around 1071 by Drogo de Beuvrière, created Lord of Holderness for his services to William the Conqueror, and became the administrative centre of the area for over a century. The 'sea' in the name of Skipsea refers to a lake, not the ocean, and Drogo may have built on a natural island rising above the surrounding water. Archaeological finds hint at the possibility of a Bronze or Iron age lake dwelling, long before the coming of the Normans.

Skipsea Castle had many advantages. It was well protected, it could repel any invaders from Europe,

Skipsea Castle.

and it probably also served as an inland port with navigable access from the sea. A dig conducted by the Humberside Archaeological Unit in 1987-8 showed that the use of boulder clay had helped to preserve the mound from substantial erosion and that it was originally two-thirds of its present height, with additional layers added as needed. The keep erected on the summit was almost certainly wooden, though the remains of a stone wall (probably of a later date) add an element of mystery to the story.

A later lord, William le Gros, established a new town under the protection of the castle some time around 1160, but it did not flourish and survives only in the name, Skipsea Brough. As for the castle itself, the end came in 1221 when Henry III ordered its destruction after another lord, William de Forz, took part in a rebellion.

In any event, by the end of the 12th century the administrative centre of Holderness moved to the royal manor at Burstwick which, unlikely though it now seems, was an establishment of such importance with its chapels, chambers and deer parks that it has been described as the medieval Sandringham of the North. All of which proves how much imagination is needed to transform humps, bumps and uneven bits of ground into the buildings which have left no other trace.

THE KING WHO CAME TO A KING'S TOWN

Henry VIII and Hull

The find of a well-preserved Tudor gun is a timely reminder of the impact Henry VIII had on Hull. When he arrived in the town on 10 September 1541 he was received with the enthusiastic welcome traditional on such occasions, though this time there was added excitement. The visit was totally unexpected, with no opportunity for the meticulous preparations which usually ensure that no blemish offends the royal eyes. The problems of travel in the 16th century made kings a rare sight in Yorkshire.

Henry, accompanied by his fifth queen, Catherine Howard, and a retinue of courtiers was given the use of the Suffolk Palace (or Manor House), later the site of the G.P.O., and the mayor, no doubt overwhelmed by it all, greeted the visitors with excessive flattery. During the three-day visit the Corporation put on lavish entertainment for the distinguished guests and earned more gratitude by the presentation of £100 to the King.

If the aldermen felt odd twinges of anxiety amid the merriment, their unease was not without cause. The visit was not so much intended as an honour to the town as a display of royal power in the North of England. Hull already had one grim symbol of Henry's treatment of those who dared to disobey. High above the Beverley Gate at the entrance to Whitefriargate hung the chained skeleton of Sir Robert Constable, one of the leaders of the Pilgrimage of Grace in 1536, the failed revolt against Henry's attack on the monasteries. Constable and other rebels were hanged at strategic points throughout the North, and the King continued his policy undeterred. In 1539 the property of three religious institutions in Hull, the Whitefriars, the Blackfriars and the Carthusians (apart from their hospital) was confiscated.

After this show of strength Henry left for York but he was back within three weeks. His arrival on 30 September coincided with the election of a new mayor and, although Alderman Johnson was the chosen candidate, he seems to have been over-awed by the course of events and declined the position. Not surprisingly, the King's own nominee, Sir John Elland, was unanimously supported as the man to take his place.

This second visit, now of added interest in view if the discovery of the gun, was the time when Henry declared his intention to make Hull 'mighty strong'. As a consequence, a fourth wall, with blockhouse and castle, was erected on the Drypool side of the River. A persistent local myth is that Henry ordered the tower of St. Mary's Church to be demolished so that he could get a better view of the shipping from his window at the Suffolk Palace, once again his temporary residence. Although he was a monarch accustomed to getting his own way and with a strong interest in maritime matters, the truth is more mundane. The original tower of St. Mary's had fallen in 1518, causing much damage, the nave was shortened, and material from the ruin was recycled in the new fortifications.

This five-day visit brought an additional benefit to Hull and Holderness. Now that there were defences on the east bank, there was an obvious need for an efficient crossing of the River, and the outmoded ferry was replaced by the first North Bridge, a short distance south of the present bridge.

After five days the King sailed across the Humber to Lincolnshire, never to return. Catherine Howard was executed the next year – and Beverley was left to fume at the hindrance to its ships caused by the bridge, a dispute which again raised its head in the more recent controversy about the new crossing of the River Hull.

WHEN ELECTORS ENJOYED ELECTIONS

Corrupt 19th-century elections

Already bored with the election?* Maybe the 19th-century version would have been more in your line.

An election then was a carnival, with candidates spending huge sums on party colours, orange for the Liberals, blue for the Tories, except in Beverley where crimson was preferred, and pink for those who wished to stress their independence. Each candidate wanted to daunt his opponents with an impressive display of popular support, and the town was awash with flags, ribbons and rosettes, and coloured cards stuck into hat bands, on carriages, whips – and even ladies' bonnets.

Free entertainment was provided by endless bands and processions, and a particular spectacle in Hull was the grand entrance of candidates, who were often met at the town's boundary by colourful armies of supporters and escorted into the centre with music and patriotic songs. To prove their commitment they would sometimes remove horses from the shafts and draw carriages along under their own manpower.

*General Election 1997.

The excitement an election generated owed at least as much to the financial benefits in store as it did to politics. Only a minority (all male) were entitled to vote, and most regarded it as perfectly normal to be paid for their support. A six-week campaign would have been seen as a golden opportunity to extract even more from candidates who had no option but to pay. Bribery and corruption flourished so vigorously because voting was not made confidential until the secret ballot was introduced in 1872 – Hull used it for the first time at a by-election in 1873 – and the publication of the poll meant that a check could be made to ensure that those paid for their promises had voted the right way.

A pleasant perk for voters, quite apart from cash payments, was the unlimited quantity of free drink and food available at an inn which kept 'open house' for those who claimed to be the supporters of a particular candidate. It was a system which lent itself to obvious abuse, and this generous flow of alcohol often ended on polling day, as it did in Hull in 1834, with 'the sight of men parading the streets in a state of intoxication, of men carried almost senseless in the cabs' on their way to register their votes.

Party rivalry could easily get out of control in this heated atmosphere. When Tory M.P. John Mitchell arrived in Hull in 1820 he and his supporters were pelted with snowballs and ice along Anlaby Road and, after he had alighted from his carriage in Lowgate, a mob completely demolished it. What they could not burn was thrown into the Humber. The proximity of the town docks was a temptation to trouble-makers. In 1832 a distinguished Liberal M.P., Matthew Hill, was attacked with paving stones and only avoided being thrown into the water with the help of a friendly hairdresser who banged his curling tongs on the assailants' knuckles.

Beverley was not excluded from its share of violent fun. In 1857 a London lawyer, who arrived with documents to prove that a popular candidate, Edmund Glover, was unqualified to stand, had to take refuge in the Akrill family's house in Saturday Market. Its windows were promptly broken, though, fortunately, heavy rain dowsed a bonfire lit outside. The lawyer was eventually allowed to leave and was lucky to escape with nothing more than a farewell salute of hoots and hisses. In 1868 a general election coincided with the Martinmas holidays in Driffield, and reinforcements of police had to be brought in to overcome a rampage of stone-throwing farm lads.

For candidates who managed to survive the ordeal and win a seat it still wasn't over. Both in Hull and Beverley the man who topped the poll was carried aloft in a ribbon-bedecked chair, round King Billy's statue in Hull and round the Market Cross in Beverley. It was a doubtful honour which some sensibly declined in view of the missiles from the opponents which greeted them in this hazardous ride. But winners and losers alike had one more score to settle: the inflated bills at the inns where votes had been so dearly bought.

150 YEARS ON

T. R. Ferens

If you travel along Holderness Road on 4 May* look across towards Holderness House. Every year on that date a flag is flown to mark the birthday of the great philanthropist, Thomas Robinson Ferens, who lived there for 20 years until his death in 1930. In 1997 Kingston upon Hull celebrates its elevation to the status of a city and it's a happy coincidence that the civic centenary falls in the same year as the 150th anniversary of the birth of a man who contributed so much to its prosperity and reputation.

Ferens was not a local boy and arrived in Hull only in 1868 when he became confidential secretary and shorthand clerk to James Reckitt. Born in New Shildon, County Durham, he had left school at 13 to work, first, for the Stockton and Darlington Railway, and six years later for an engineering company. Stories about him abound. One tradition is that his beautifully written letter of application so impressed Reckitt that he was the automatic choice for the advertised post. Another is that he arrived in Hull with only half a crown in his pocket.

*1997

T. R. Ferens.

The facts certainly prove that his outstanding talent was immediately recognised. He was brilliant at shorthand and, as a staunch Wesleyan, kept in practice on Sundays by taking down the sermons. Older people recall how he always stressed the importance of shorthand when he spoke to them as schoolchildren, and pointed to his own career as evidence of its value. His progress at Reckitt's was a shining example of what could be achieved by ability and hard work, and he climbed confidently up the ladder of promotion to become Works Manager, Secretary, General Manager, Director and, in due course, Chairman.

Those who knew him are left with the memory of a man who was always smart and upright and who expected from employees the high standards he set himself. A stickler for punctuality, he was often in his office by 6 am, he disliked any sign of waste, and he was a convinced teetotaller. Photographs show a serious face, though one story told about him indicates that he could see the lighter side of life. He had given a young employee a letter to deliver and, seeing him take his time, told him to run. The boy's reply, 'I don't get running wages, sir,' appealed to his sense of humour.

Although he had no family, he was happily married to Esther Ellen Field, daughter of a well-known Hull merchant and grocer, William Field, and both Mr. and Mrs. Ferens loved teaching the children of the Brunswick Chapel Sunday School.

It was a great day for him when, in the Liberal landslide of 1906, he was elected M.P. for East Hull at his second attempt. He retained the seat until 1918. As an important public figure he was increasingly loaded with honours. Hull made him a freeman and, well respected at Westminster, he was appointed a Privy Councillor in 1912 and so entitled to be described as 'The Rt. Hon. T. R. Ferens'.

But it is his munificence to the City which has ensured him a unique place in its history. His gifts included land for East Park boating lake and the YPI Recreation Ground, and he participated in the foundation of the Garden Village. Determined that Hull should have the cultural and educational facilities it deserved, he donated land and substantial sums of money to create the Ferens Art Gallery, and a site on Cottingham Road and £¼ million of Reckitt's shares for building what is now the University of Hull.

Holderness House itself was left as a home of rest for gentlewomen, and residents have the privilege of retirement in a most graceful setting. It stands discreetly in its own grounds away from the main road, as unostentatious as its former owner, but this year the flag flown on his birthday has every right to flutter with extra pride.

Holderness House.

THE BLUNT BENEFACTOR

Christopher Pickering

Christopher Pickering's gift to the City of the park opened in 1911 rarely makes the headlines, but a recent debate about his donation has provided an opportunity for putting the spotlight once again on a man who for most local people is now merely a name.

'Kit' Pickering, as he was usually known, was a type our Victorian ancestors admired: a self-made man who started with nothing and made a fortune through sheer hard work and business acumen. His achievement is even more remarkable than the career of T. R. Ferens, as Pickering came from a much humbler background. Born in 1842, he had the most basic education before he started to earn his own living at the age of 10. In the heyday of his later prosperity he recalled that his first job was in Mr. Self's fish-curing house in Finkle Street; the work was hard and the wage one shilling (5p) a week with board included.

He stayed there for two years and then moved to Mr. (later Alderman) Fountain's herring-curing establishment, where he remained 13 or 14 years. Still in his twenties, he thought the time was ripe to be his own boss, and he set up as a fish salesman, a middleman, buying and re-selling fish from the smacks which sailed into Hull. The next crucial stage was to buy his own smack, the *George Peabody*, and, as success bred success, he built up a fleet.

A man who aims to make a fortune has to be alert to the wind of change. Steam was to make the wind-powered smacks obsolete, and, at a time when many smack owners were facing bankruptcy, Pickering disposed of his vessels and risked his precarious capital by ordering four steam trawlers. 'It is the steam trawlers that have made the fishing industry so great a feature in the trade of Hull,' he claimed, and took obvious pride in his role in this phenomenal expansion.

In spite of his growing wealth and importance in the business community, Kit Pickering, everyone agreed, 'never pretended to be anything that he was not'. A true Yorkshireman, he disliked ' display and ostentation' and 'there was no mistaking what he meant when he spoke his mind'. His actions were proof of his courage and independence, but, while most admired his 'honest, rugged, fearless nature', there were those who commented less enthusiastically that he was 'generously endowed with the attributes that make for material success'.

Christopher Pickering.

Founder of Pickering and Haldane's Steam Trawling Company and eventually director and chairman of so many companies that he wielded considerable power in the fishing industry, he remained loyal to West Hull until the late 1890s when he moved from 114 Coltman Street to Hornsea, in 1897 taking over the home formerly occupied by the railway entrepreneur, J.A. Wade, since demolished and now the site of Hornsea School.

Financial success enabled him to plough back a substantial part of his fortune into the area where it had been earned. An old gentleman who worked in Hull's Victorian Town Hall had vivid memories of Kit Pickering handing him a bag of sovereigns which he intended as another donation, and, in his typically blunt way, ordering him to 'Count that, lad!'

It is for Pickering Park that he is best remembered. Hull was a pioneer of botanical gardens and public parks, and Pickering Park had a number of features that were modern for their time. Instead of the over-disciplined regimentation of many parks, the landscaping was designed with great vision so that the layout appeared as natural as possible, and Pickering was progressive too in his wish for the park to contain plenty of space for sports and games.

He died at his Hornsea home in 1920, a man who did not mince his words and who would, one suspects, have had something vigorous to add to any discussion on Pickering Park.

THE POINT ABOUT SAMMY

Sammy's Point

'Who or what was Sammy's Point named after?' asked a recent correspondent to the *Hull Daily Mail.*

There really was a Sammy, though this was rather a disrespectful way of referring to Martin Samuelson, an important civic figure in 19th-century Hull and a leading shipbuilder whose 12-acre premises on the east side of the River Hull near its junction with the Humber became popularly known as Sammy's Point.

Born in Hamburg in 1825, Samuelson worked as a railway engineer before moving to Hull in 1849 and taking over an iron foundry in Scott Street. The business grew and, being a typical Victorian entrepreneur, ever alert to new opportunities, he expanded into iron shipbuilding in 1853, with his first vessel, the *Irwell*, launched the following year. His shipyards were enlarged to include part of the old Citadel, and the quantity of modern machinery and the advantages of the vast site with access to both the Hull and the Humber made it one of the country's finest shipbuilding establishments. By 1859 around 40 ships had been built and later the total was approaching 100. 'The River Hull,' it was said, 'bristled with iron ships in various stages of completion', and his weekly wage bill rose to a staggering £1,200.

What about the man himself? Samuelson, still only in his 30s in this exciting period of prosperity, made

Sammy's Point.

quite an impression with his small, compact figure and his black bushy whiskers, his lively dark eyes and his colourful clothes, white hat, blue coat and light trousers. A bundle of energy, he seemed to exist without sleep, and he was a familiar sight dashing along the streets of Hull: 'At one hour he is at the building yard in Groves, a few minutes later and he is inspecting the docking of a ship, half an hour more and he has visited both the boiler works in Church Street and the engine works in Scott Street.'

A man who was so keen to thrust ahead had no time for those who tried to thwart his plans. On one occasion, when he had contracted to have ships ready on a given day, he made an agreement with his workforce that anyone who left without permission or notice should forfeit a certain sum. The joiners later went on strike but, rather than be pressurised into increasing their wages, he called their bluff and enforced the penalty and brought in outside labour.

Like other captains of industry in that period he regarded it as his duty to play his part in public affairs, and served as alderman and mayor, with a particular concern for improving Hull's sanitation. But the high point of his public career was the day in 1863 when the former Lord Goderich, unseated for corruption after his election as a Hull MP in 1852, but now the inheritor of two sonorous titles, returned in ironic triumph as Earl de Grey and Ripon for his installation as Lord High Steward. At dawn a distinguished party and thousands of spectators watched the spectacular launch of four ships from Samuelson's yard, after which he entertained his guests to a champagne breakfast and heard himself toasted 'in most complimentary terms' by the Earl.

It was not to be a story with a happy ending. Rumours were spreading that Samuelson was overreaching himself and he was further damaged by the bankruptcy of the shipowner, Zachariah Pearson. He too was declared bankrupt, resigned as alderman, and was compelled to sell his business. As the storm clouds gathered, however, a touching tribute was paid by his employees who presented him with 'a silver tea and coffee service, two silver salvers and a beautiful timepiece' as a token of their esteem.

The great days were over, but, when he died in 1903 at the age of 78, he was still in harness, working as engineer for the Humber Conservancy. Martin Samuelson never had a minute to spare and it was characteristic of the man that he was on the telephone talking to one of his clerks only half an hour before his death.

PICTURES AND PORK SAUSAGES
The Hohenrein Family

The Regal cinemas in Beverley* and Hull have a decidedly unregal appearance as they stand dilapidated and forlorn, a sad memorial to a remarkable local man, Charles H. Ross, a director of the company which built the two Regals and the royal family of cinemas, the Regis, the Rex and the Royalty, in the 1930s.

Mr. Ross was born in 1883, but, until he was in his thirties, his surname was Hohenrein. His father, George Friederick Hohenrein, had arrived in Hull in 1848 as a 16-year-old immigrant. For two years he worked for a German pork butcher in Mytongate, and then, with amazing self-confidence for a teenager in a foreign country, opened his own shop at 7 Waterworks Street, on a site where Queen's House, Paragon Street, now stands. On Sundays he attended the German Lutheran church and there, one supposes, he met his future wife, Katharine Meyer, a domestic servant who spoke no English.

The business prospered and his proud claim was that 'Hohenrein's sausages are the best'. A second shop was opened at 22 Princes Avenue and the family settled

---

*The Regal, Beverley, has since been demolished, to be replaced by apartments and shops.

G. William Hohenrein, elder brother of Charles H. Hohenrein (Ross).

On his departure on 1907 the running of the business passed to his younger brother, Charles, who in 1911 married a local girl, Lily Westwood. The shop continued to thrive, and the future looked bright. But international events were to have a devastating effect on this loyal British family. In the summer of 1914 Charles was visiting William in Germany and just managed to get home safely as war was declared. As an alien resident in an enemy country, however, William and his son, a medical student, were interned in a concentration camp and their suffering was intense. Charles, back in Hull, was eager to do his bit and, although declared unfit when he volunteered for the army, served as a sergeant in a civilian corps.

His devotion to the British cause was total, but the bombardment of Scarborough, the sinking of the *Lusitania*, and the first Zeppelin raid on Hull inflamed patriotism to the point of hysteria. Mobs marched on the premises of innocent people whose reputation as model citizens was no excuse for a German surname, and the Hohenreins were not exempt from these nasty attacks of window-breaking and destruction. So intolerable did the situation become that Charles, wearied by 'daily insults, base insinuations and threats', had no alternative but to close his business until the war clouds cleared. There was one other significant change. Like the Royal family, who became Windsors, Charles rid himself of his fateful handicap and adopted the name, Ross.

Things were never the same again in Germany, and a crowning irony came in the Second World War when William's son, now a doctor and on duty, was killed in an Allied raid. For the brother, now Charles H. Ross, it was a time to forget. He took an increasingly important part in local business and sporting life, and his role as a cinema magnate was just one of many activities in a crowded life. The Waterworks Street shop, damaged during the Blitz, was demolished after his retirement. The business moved, but the name, Ross, still surviving on a stall in the Market Hall, gives no hint of its dramatic history.

in a comfortable home, Derringham Cottage, off Spring Bank. Most important of all, G.F. Hohenrein became a naturalised British citizen, for the family regarded themselves as Hullensians to the core and were as patriotically English as it was possible to be.

When he died the business was taken over by his eldest son, William, whose German wife, Julie, was in poor health. Reluctantly, on medical advice, he agreed to settle with her in Germany, a considerable sacrifice as he saw it as a strange foreign country, and thereafter looked forward longingly to his annual visit to 'Hull, the city of my nativity'.

THE KING WHO DID NOT LOSE HIS SPURS

William III

The Old Town, according to a recent report, is to have a £75,000 face-lift, good news not only for local people who value this piece of living history but also for visitors who are often amazed to find such a fascinating area so near a modern city centre. Nothing surprises them more than the gleaming golden equestrian statue of William III, now regarded with great affection as the unofficial symbol of Hull itself but which has had quite a rocky ride since it was erected in 1734.

The reason for the decision to erect a statue is revealed in the inscription describing William as 'Our Great Deliverer'. His predecessor, the Catholic James II, was heartily disliked in Protestant Hull, particularly for demanding the surrender of its charter and replacing hostile aldermen with his own nominees. After he had lost his throne in the Glorious Revolution of 1688 a rumour that Catholics were to take control of the garrison so alarmed the Protestants that they seized the Citadel and overpowered the Governor, the Catholic Lord Langdale, on 4 December 1688, henceforth always known as Town Taking Day.

Hull people have an eye for a bargain and, when Bristol held a competition for the design of a statue of William, the opportunity came. The entry submitted by sculptor Michael Rysbrack was selected and that of Peter Scheemakers dismissed as 'competent but a little devoid of character'. It was, however, good enough for Hull and purchased for £893. 10s. 0d.

What could be a more fitting day for 'opening' the statue than the anniversary of Town Taking Day? And so, on 4 December 1734 anybody who was anybody processed to the Market Place. Buildings around were illuminated and the people of Hull equally lit up as they repeatedly drank to King William's memory 'till they lost their own'.

The statue, cast in lead and pewter, was rather sombre until it was first gilded in 1768, and by then its

King Billy in the Market Place.

68

location in the centre of the town's busiest commercial area had caused problems. Carts and carriages knocked against it and, although protective railing was added, its four corner-stones hindered traffic and the square was reduced to an octagon. Repairs were necessary on a number of occasions but it held its ground when there was talk of a move to a less hazardous site. At some point Jacobites are said to have removed a thistle formerly under the horse's hoof as they could not bear to see it trample on such a powerful Scottish symbol, and a golden crown presented by the Jewish population had to be removed to a safer place.

One myth must be dispelled. Scheemakers did not forget to add spurs and stirrups. He based his design on the statue of Emperor Marcus Aurelius in Rome, portraying William in Roman dress and sandals. On a work of art in classical style such extras were not necessary. Nor did he commit suicide when he discovered his 'mistake'. He died perfectly naturally in 1781.

Repairs and re-gilding in recent years have made King Billy as grand as he ever was. Experts tend to agree that he is inferior to Rysbrack's King and describe him as sitting 'stiffly upright with a slightly anxious expression on his face'. Local people, however, ignore such insults and see William as a fine figure of a man and his appearance 'easy and graceful' as his horse raises a hoof in eternally suspended animation.

There is one ironic footnote to the saga. In the last war King Billy was evacuated to Houghton Hall near Market Weighton and given refuge by Colonel Philip Langdale, descendant of the Governor who had been overthrown when the people of Hull made it clear that they preferred William III to James II.

FROM TOP TO BOTTOM

Joseph Walker Pease

The sad story of Joseph Walker Pease should be a warning to newly-elected M.P.s of the hazards of a political career.

A chance to enter Parliament came in 1873 when he was already 53, living in some style at Hesslewood Hall, the head of an influential East Riding family since the death of his father, the banker and industrialist, Joseph Robinson Pease. His privileged background guaranteed him a prominent place in the local community, but the death of the long-serving Liberal M.P. for Hull, James Clay, on 26 September 1873, created an opportunity he was unable to resist. Clay had been an excellent constituency M.P. but his halo was beginning to slip as he neared the end of his career, and many thought it was time for a change. For the Conservative Pease there was every prospect of capturing the seat in the ensuing by-election.

It was a short campaign, with excitement in both camps as the Liberal candidate, Edward J. Reed, believed that he had an equally good chance of holding on to this traditionally Liberal seat. Polling day, 22 October, was an historic occasion: the first time Hull electors voted by secret ballot, a reform introduced the previous year to end the corruption of open voting when bribers could check on the bribed. Fascinated by the novelty, the press reported at length how voters obtained new ballot papers and then retired to 'a small closet guarded by a policeman'.

Confidentiality about the state of the poll took away much of the customary noise and commotion, but no one could be unaware that an election was in progress. Party colours, blue for Tory and orange for Liberal, were displayed in shop windows, and ships in the harbour and docks were dressed with flags of the appropriate shade. People had few inhibitions about revealing their allegiance, and, as well as the usual ribbons and cards, there were some original touches. One rullyman had decorated his horse's head with blue cards and ribbons and tied its tail in orange ribbons to indicate his expectation of the result. Astute voters had realised that the secret ballot made it possible to start a new electoral tradition, riding to the polls in opponents' transport, and the Tory press attacked Liberals who hid their colours and travelled in Conservative carriages.

Polling closed at 4 pm, but a count was another innovation, and what would now take an hour or so lasted until 3.30 the next morning. Though the news leaked out, the official declaration did not come until 1 pm with Pease polling 6873, a majority of 279 over Reed. After making his victory speech from the upper window of the George Hotel he left Hull, and 'the whole village of Hessle' turned out to welcome the returning hero. The church bells rang and his carriage was hauled

by 25 loyal supporters preceded by a large blue device with the message in gilt letters, 'Welcome to Colonel Pease. M.P. for Hull'. Pease expressed his gratitude, the horses were returned to their shafts and the victor rode on to Hesslewood 'while the air rang again with true British cheers'.

It was to be a short-lived triumph. The by-election took place during the long autumn-winter recess which Parliament enjoyed in more leisurely days. Before he could take his seat, Parliament was dissolved on 26 January 1874, and in the general election on 4 February Pease came bottom of the poll. His political career was over. He had been an M.P. for three months without an opportunity of even sitting in the Chamber of the Commons.

PAGANS AND PRIESTS

Goodmanham

1997, the year which marks the 1,400th anniversary of the arrival of St. Augustine in Kent, is a good time to focus on a local village church which has an honoured place in the next chapter in the story: how Christianity came from Kent to Yorkshire.

The village is Goodmanham, where All Hallows Church stands on a mound, an important factor in its history. Pagan temples (probably wooden structures, far less grand than they sound) were often erected on high points of land, and it was Augustine's sensible belief that the transition to Christianity would be easier for converts to accept if familiar places of worship were retained by the new religion.

Augustine was sent on his mission by Pope Gregory, and older readers will remember being taught how it all began. The Pope, it was said, had been moved by the sight of captive fair-haired children, and, on discovering where they came from, had declared that they were 'not Angles but Angels', too good to be

All Hallows Church, Goodmanham.

brought up in heathen ways. Whatever the truth of this attractive story, it was certainly Gregory who in 596 despatched Augustine, with a small band of monks, on his missionary task. The following year he landed in Kent, was given permission to preach, established a church and converted the King, Ethelbert.

The story now moves to East Yorkshire. In 625 Edwin, King of Northumbria (literally all the area north of the Humber) married the daughter of Ethelbert, a Kentish princess with the unlovely name of Ethelberga, who was already a Christian, and brought with her Paulinus, her chaplain, to her husband's estate, presumed to be in the Londesborough area. Edwin apparently spent two years pondering the possibility of adopting his wife's religion, and in 627 called a meeting in his hall at Londesborough which had far-reaching consequences.

What happened next was described by the first English historian, Bede (who had been ordained by the Bishop who became St. John of Beverley). Paulinus explained the central truths of the religion he taught, but it was an anonymous old pagan priest who brought the assembly to its historic climax. Describing a scene with which everyone was familiar, he compared the life of a man to a bird flying out of the darkness into the light and warmth of the hall before flying off again into the dark unknown. Paulinus, he said, had given a convincing answer to the greatest mystery of all: where we come from and where we go. His sincerity so inspired the pagan high priest, Coifi, that he mounted a stallion and rode to the nearest pagan temple, which he and his followers demolished, burning what remained.

Bede gives the location of this building as Godmundingaham, which no one seriously doubts is the present Goodmanham. Augustine's insistence on easing the way for converts makes it highly likely that worship continued on the same site, but in a new church and according to the rites of the new religion.

Coifi's dramatic action led to the conversion of King Edwin, and on Easter Day 627 he was baptised, some say at Pocklington, others at York. It was York which clearly benefited most from the King's decision. Paulinus was given a site formerly occupied by the Roman legions and established a simple wooden church which over the centuries and with much rebuilding became York Minster.

Goodmanham was never to become so grand or so famous; but it was important enough for the present church to be erected in the 12th century as an improvement on whatever building previously occupied the site. Many changes have taken place during the following 800 years, but its Norman tower, one of the finest in the East Riding, stands on the mound as solidly as ever, a powerful reminder of the significance of Paulinus's journey to Yorkshire.

DENMARK AND WONDERLAND

St. Mary's Church, Beverley

St. Mary's Church, Beverley, impresses some tourists so much that they assume it must be the Minster. Its grandeur is obvious but interest does not depend solely on size, and St. Mary's has two features with a particular fascination for visitors.

Those who stroll along Hengate and look across to the southern side of the church are usually intrigued but puzzled by a rhyming epitaph which is not too easy to read as the old-fashioned 'f' is used for an 's'. Below crossed swords is the surprising information:

> Here Two young Danish soldiers lye
> The one in quarrell chanc'd to die
> The other's Head by their own Law
> With Sword was sever'd at one Blow
> December the 23rd 1689

William III (the King Billy, whose Hull statue was

Memorial to the Danish soldiers.

December 16 1689 Daniel Straker, a Danish trooper buried
December 23 1689 Johannes Frederick Bellow, a Danish trooper beheaded for killing the other, buried.

But much more vivid is an eye-witness account of the execution which the distinguished Beverley historian, Ken MacMahon, quoted as an example of the way the centuries can be breached when elderly people pass on to the young the things they have been told in their own childhood. A girl, Mary Hopwood, saw the execution in the Market Place, and all her life remembered the dark day and the wagons of gravel brought in for an obvious purpose. She lived to be 104 and passed on the story to her daughter, who lived to be 80. She told a neighbour who also lived to a ripe old age, and she in turn told a man who apparently wrote to the *Hull Daily Mail* on the subject.

Most visitors come across the epitaph by chance, but many go inside to search for the White Rabbit – not easy to spot, but in the north-east of the church, on the right-hand side of the door from St. Michael's Chapel to the Sacristy. Its similarity to the picture of the White Rabbit in *Alice in Wonderland* is so striking that many believe it was the model used by the artist, John Tenniel. There is, however, no conclusive proof, only circumstantial evidence. The real name of 'Lewis Carroll', the author of *Alice*, was the Rev. Charles Lutwidge Dodgson, whose grandfather, Charles Lutwidge, held the important post of Collector of Customs in Hull and lived at one to the town's best addresses, 7 Charlotte Street. His house stood in what is now George Street, in the space between the Queen's Hotel and the YPI, and the author's parents were married in Hull.

There was every reason for 'Lewis Carroll' to come to Hull to visit relations and, as a clergyman, to visit St. Mary's but the most positive information available is that a descendant to Tenniel states 'quite firmly' that his artist ancestor was sent to Beverley by Carroll. Unless new facts emerge, the verdict this time must be 'Quite probable but not proven.'

the subject of a recent article) was the reason for the presence of these two Danes in Beverley. They were mercenaries, ready to fight for a foreign king for payment, and, according to a Danish historian who has researched the subject, were in a large troop of fellow countrymen who had been recruited to serve William in his campaign in Ireland. After landing in Hull, they were stationed in Beverley, awaiting orders.

As the epitaph shows, it was just before Christmas when the incident occurred. 'They loved strong drink,' says a contemporary diarist, and it may well have been that they were enjoying a seasonal tipple when high spirits led to a brawl which ended in a death. Whatever the circumstances, one man died and his assailant was executed, the documentary proof being entries in the parish register:

CROSSING THE HUMBER'S TROUBLED WATERS

Humber Ferries

A walk to the Pier was once a regular routine for Hull people: an innocent pleasure permitted on a day when other entertainment was taboo – and with the added benefits of healthy exercise and fresh air to fill your lungs. On other days the horse-wash was always something to watch, as well as the main focus of interest, the departure (with a terrifyingly loud hoot) and arrival of the New Holland Ferry.

It was an even busier area in earlier times, not merely a spot to stand and stare but an important part of the town's communication system, when rivers were regarded less as barriers than as means of travel and transport preferable to the inferior roads. Edward I (the man who put the 'King' into 'Kingston') established a ferry from Barton to Hull in 1315 and later the town acquired the right to operate the service for an annual fee, and eventually sublet this right. By the 19th century Hull also controlled the Barton-Hessle ferry, financial arrangements which led to a major crisis when this monopolistic power was challenged.

Many will remember the attempts of Lord Noel-Buxton to prove that the Roman legions had forded the Humber. He was not entirely successful, and there's plenty of evidence to show that even crossing by boat had its dangers. In 1641 the Rev. Andrew Marvell, father of the poet of the same name, was drowned on such a journey, and in 1697 the pioneering tourist, Celia Fiennes,

wrote that the Humber 'rolls and tosses just like the sea, only the soil being clay turns the water and waves yellow, and so it differs from the sea in colour, not else'. James Boswell, biographer of Dr. Johnson, found the crossing a 'disagreeable, tacking passage' when he sailed over to Hull in 1778.

In the pre-railway period the ferry terminal was the point at which people and mail began their long journey to London, and 19th-century directories give details of the times when passengers could take the Royal Mail or the Express Post Coach from Barton Waterside. In 1802 William Wordsworth and his sister,

Victoria Pier, Hull

Valentines Seri

73

Dorothy, used this service en route from North Yorkshire, and although Dorothy was scathing about Hull ('a frightful, dirty, brick housy, tradesmanlike, rich, vulgar place'), she was captivated by the view of the river, which 'looked beautiful with the evening lights upon it and boats moving about'.

The tranquillity was rudely shattered when a Radical agitator, James Acland, arrived in Hull, in 1831. He quickly latched on to popular discontent about the ferry services and drew attention to the high profits made by the Corporation and its lessees, pointing out that the Crown grant of 1315 had specified a half-penny return fare for a foot passenger: any increase was illegal. As a challenge he hired a boat, named it *Public Opinion* and displayed the town's arms upside down. There was great excitement as thousands flocked to his support and this competition so affected income from the authorised ferry service that legal action was taken against him at the York Assizes. By this time Hull Corporation was understandably weary of the whole business and probably relieved when a much quicker service was started between New Holland and Hull. Barton complained, but the New Holland Ferry only ended with the opening of the Humber Bridge.

The shabby state of the Pier and its environs, which lasted so long into the post-war years, has now been replaced by a most attractive scheme of paving and architectural restoration. It is true that the booking office which once had the rare distinction of being a railway station without trains is now without tickets, but it's as pleasant a place as it was in 1891 when a guide book asked rhetorically; 'Where, away from the sea, is there such another noble expanse of water?'

WEDNESDAY MARKET SETS OUT ITS STALLS

Wednesday Market, Beverley

Wednesday Market is no longer open only on Saturdays: the confusing state of affairs which mystified visitors before the re-opening of Beverley's oldest market place on the 'proper' day of the week.

Churches and markets tend to go hand in hand. Pilgrims visiting the tomb of St. John of Beverley in the Minster looked for food, drink and accommodation as well as the fulfilment of their spiritual needs, and this medieval form of tourism led to the provision of hostelries, shops and stalls where they could satisfy their material wants.

Originally Wednesday Market would begin at the walls of the Minster, but later there was infilling of the open area with the building of Eastgate and Highgate, and the market became distanced from the church.

It was a busy place, handy for goods brought along the River Hull and the Beck, but the growth of Beverley in a northerly direction left it in the wake of progress and it was the more central Saturday Market which became the main trading area. By the 1730s Wednesday Market was on its last legs. It remained, though, a place of communal activities with its own market cross, (later rebuilt as an obelisk and only demolished in 1881), and with more grisly items – stocks, a pillory house and a cockpit.

The weekly market had ended long before the arrival in about 1770 of young Mary Wollstonecraft, who grew up to be a pioneering feminist, the mother of the writer of *Frankenstein*, and the mother-in-law of the poet, Shelley. Records confirm that Mary's father paid rates on a house in Wednesday Market but its exact location is unknown. The Wollstonecrafts were in Beverley for only six years, long enough, however, for Mary to decide that Georgian Beverley was not to her taste. Her father's drinking and violent temper caused the neighbours to gossip and, when she returned as an adult after a tempestuous career, she was appalled to find many of them still living the same lives in the same houses.

Mary Wollstonecraft's opinion was not generally shared. The 1871 census shows Wednesday Market as a pleasant place, even without its mid-week stalls, but with an agreeable mixture of shopkeepers, tradesmen and private residents. One of the largest businesses was owned by John Ward, printer and newspaper proprietor, who employed two men and four apprentices, three of his sons working in the family business as reporter, clerk and apprentice printer. All that has gone, but a re-assuring sign of continuity is the survival of the Queens Head, in 1871 kept by a Beverley-born innkeeper, John Turnbull.

The enclosed character of Wednesday Market was partly lost when the railway came to Beverley in 1846 and a splendid avenue, Railway Street, was cut through to give access to the station. In 1909 increasing road traffic led to the demand for an alternative route to the town centre, and part of Highgate House was lopped off to make way for Lord Roberts Road. The larger part of this elegant house remains (now occupied by Lockings) but nearby property has certainly felt the wind of change. The Primitive Methodist Chapel, erected in 1868, was replaced in the late 1950s by Crystal Garage, which in turn has given way to Boyes. The revival of the long-defunct market is still further proof that nothing stays the same for ever.

A PLACE TO PARK

The Citadel and Pearson Park

Pearson Park would never have come into existence if an earlier, ambitious plan had come to fruition.

The rapid growth of population and the loss of the fields through street building had led many to realise that a public park would be an considerable asset to the town, and from the first years of Victoria's reign the search was on for a suitable site. Attention increasingly focused on one place which seemed to offer everything that advocates of the scheme were looking for. The Citadel on the Drypool side of the River was abandoned by the military in 1848, and members of the Council became starry-eyed and their imaginations ran riot as they visualised this 'place of war and

The Lake in Pearson Park.

75

warriors' being 'devoted to the relaxation of weary minds and bodies', an idyllic spot where 'tiny children should look safely out of old embrasures, and cricket balls roll where cannon balls were piled of old'.

The site had one further advantage with a particular appeal to economy-minded councillors. They believed that, as it was no longer needed by the army, it should revert to the town without charge, and a public meeting 'numerously attended' by a galaxy of influential local men was held at the Town Hall in June 1858 in support of a petition to the Government asking for the restoration of the property.

The Court of Chancery, however, ruled against Hull's claim. The land was sold and Martin Samuelson acquired some of it for his shipyard, the Sammy's Point which was the subject of a recent article. At the same time Hull Dock Company obtained the moat, filled it in and converted it into a timber quay for Victoria Dock.

This crushing blow to Hull's hopes was the perfect opportunity for Zachariah Charles Pearson, Mayor 1859-60, to crown his mayoralty with an act of such apparent generosity that it would ensure him a permanent place on the town's roll of honour. Still in his thirties, he had enjoyed a meteoric rise to success as shipowner, merchant and civic leader, and in a dramatic gesture he purchased 37 acres of land and presented the central 27 acres to Hull for making a people's park. He retained 10 acres on the perimeter for development, and, when financial disaster later overwhelmed him, he explained in the Bankruptcy Court that he had struck a good bargain as the Council had contracted to build a road which enhanced the value of his own land. 'I do not call it giving,' he said, 'for it cost me nothing.'

The whole point of a people's park was that entrance was free. There was already the exclusive Botanic Gardens on Anlaby Road, and it was fortunate that its Curator, James Craig Niven, a landscape gardener of outstanding ability, was the man commissioned to design Pearson Park. A hand-written letter sent by him on 17 February 1860 to the Public Park Committee

(now in Kingston upon Hull Record Office) is a fascinating document, outlining the principles of his plan. To create interest at low cost he intended to introduce 'an irregular stretch of water . . . rather more than an acre in extent', and he looked to the future: 'The beauty of the trees now about to be planted will be most highly appreciable by those who are spared to enjoy their genial shade some fifty years hence.'

The grand opening on 27 August 1860 was the greatest day in Pearson's life. In 1862, however, when he was Mayor for a second term, reckless speculation and a foolhardy attempt to break the blockade of ports imposed during the American Civil War resulted in his total ruin. Yet, out of the debris of bluff, recklessness and personal tragedy, Hull acquired a fine park which guaranteed Pearson a measure of the immortality he craved.

A CITY TO SAVOUR
Hull's Architecture

Hull people need lose no sleep over the derogatory comments in a new guide (*Lonely Planet: Britain*) which dismisses the City as 'less than inspiring' and 'not a particularly attractive place'. On the contrary, when you mention Hull in other parts of the country, you often find that visitors were amazed to discover that it wasn't the stereotyped northern industrial town of belching chimneys and pungent smells they had expected. Instead, many have lasting memories of welcoming approach roads, attractive with flowers and trees, a reminder of Hull's long tradition of expertly designed public gardens.

No one would pretend that Hull is another Venice, but the celebrated architectural authority, Nikolaus Pevsner, wrote flatteringly about the Guildhall (built 1904-16) and particularly its Alfred Gelder Street facade 'which,' he said 'would look convincing in an Italian city'. Barmston Drain is no Grand Canal, yet Hull retains unmistakable evidence of its maritime origin. No discerning stranger with an ounce of imagination who stands in Nelson Street looking across the swirling waters of the Humber – and feeling the force of the wind – could fail to respond to the strong and distinctive atmosphere of a town which grew from two hamlets, Myton and Wyke, in the corner of land where two rivers meet.

The critical guide acknowledges that Hull suffered badly in the Second World War, but apparently names only Wilberforce House as a building worth seeing in High Street. No mention of Maister House, re-built after a disastrous fire in 1743, with a magnificent Palladian staircase, or of Blaydes House, with its elegant interior.

Ivan and Elisabeth Hall's book, *Georgian Hull*, revealed the quantity of fine workmanship from Hull's

The northern end of High Street.

golden age which had miraculously survived the bombs. The gently curving Prince Street (*c.*1771), viewed through its arched entrance, must be one of the most photographed places in Hull, an ideal location for filming an 18th-century play; Parliament Street has an imposing terrace of dignified houses; and no list of Hull's treasures could omit Trinity House (described by Defoe as 'the glory of the town') with its proudly ornate entrance in Trinity House Lane.

Parliament Street was built 1797-1801 as a link to Queen's Dock, opened in 1778. Too far inland, and unsuitable for modern ships, in 1935 it was filled in, but the loss of this historic dock gave Hull an asset which would otherwise have been unattainable: a central park, Queens Gardens. The view across the Gardens from Wilberforce Drive proves that Hull is a city of domes. Most imposing of all are the triple domes of the Dock Offices (1867-71), now the excellent Maritime Museum. Just beyond is the dome of the City Hall (1903-9), and to the left the domes of the Crown Court, a stylish building successfully combining the traditional and the modern.

Though individual buildings have their special features, it's the totality which creates the personality of a street. The Land of Green Ginger is one of the most famous streets in Britain and it's at the heart of a maze of alleys, lanes and courts and so many lawyers' offices that it possesses a Dickensian air. This is the point the new guide misses. Hull has its black spots and its problems (though it has avoided the worst of the 1960s' architecture which has blighted other cities), but it's a place of strong character and attractions which often have to be sought out and savoured. The writer of the new guidebook should give it a second – and a longer – look.

KING SENDS A MESSAGE FROM THE QUEEN

Queen Victoria's Diamond Jubilee, 1897: Hull becomes a city

East Yorkshire was the scene of great jollifications a hundred years ago this week. The occasion, the Diamond Jubilee celebrating the 60 years of Queen Victoria's reign, was the rarest of royal events and even the smallest villages were determined not to be outdone. Kilnsea did 'all that its big neighbours were doing', and 'the pretty little village of Kirkella', still very rural, 'was quite *en fête* for two days'.

Most programmes followed some variation on a theme of procession, sports, tea, entertainment and bonfire, but some were distinctly novel. At Atwick there were 40 sporting events which included a washing competition for women and, presumably with a prize worth catching, a hunt attracting 10 male entrants to a chase after a pig. It got out of the field and 'galloped off in grand style, giving the competitors a capital run for nearly an hour'.

Watching a colourful procession was a less demanding form of entertainment, and Hornsea put on an impressive parade composed of all the town's dignitaries and organisations one would expect, but also with five adult and three juvenile members of the United Ancient Order of Druids on six horses and two donkeys, in Druidic garb and carrying banners. Forty gaily-decorated cyclists brought up the rear.

Two facts shine through the press reports of these celebrations: the community spirit which flourished in the pre-television age, with virtually everybody ready to join in, and the sheer pleasure derived from the simplest forms of entertainment. There was no mincing of words to ensure political correctness, and Driffield was one of many places where a tea was given to the 'aged and poor'. Each Driffield 'scholar', too, was treated to sandwiches, cakes and 'cooling drinks', a much appreciated item on the menu. Queen Victoria was usually lucky with her weather, the Diamond Jubilee was celebrated in overpowering heat, and organisers of outdoor events were grateful for this typical spell of 'Queen's weather'.

Much of the Victorian memorabilia which fetches high prices in antique shops had its origin in these village events. At Brantingham the children were presented with Jubilee mugs, and at a more commercially-minded Burstwick tea ended with the Jubilee pots and plates being sold by auction. They were eagerly bought up by people from nearby villages who wanted them for their own celebrations.

Inhabitants of Brough and Elloughton were greeted by a rendition of the National Anthem from Mr. Sapcote on his postman's horn as he started his round, and early in the morning the bells of Driffield church began a merry peal. They continued all day, and perhaps residents had had enough by evening, though they were luckier than the people of Cottingham, whose bells had been sent away for restoration: 'As the time drew nigh and the bells were not delivered, the firm were reminded of their completing their contract in time for the Jubilee'. The Rector and churchwardens, it was pointed out, were not at fault.

For Hull there was a double celebration. While a thanksgiving service was being held in Holy Trinity Church on Sunday, 20 June, a telegram from Sir Seymour King, M.P. for Central Hull, announced that the Queen was to grant Hull the status of a city. As his own contribution to the festivities he provided the children of his constituents with coupons which they could exchange for free ice-cream, and crowds were seen besieging the ice-cream man's 'truck' on Anlaby Road. After the 1910 election the Courts decided that King's extreme generosity to electors amounted to corruption, and he was deprived of his seat. Many years later his offence is largely forgotten, but in 1997 Hull has good reason to remember the contents of that famous telegram.

ONE MAN'S CENTURY

Thomas Leak

Queen Victoria's Diamond Jubilee was a once-in-a-lifetime event, but in 1897 there was one man in Hull who had vivid memories of the Golden Jubilee of Victoria's grandfather, George III.

He was Thomas Leak, then in his 100th year, and surely qualifying as a Hullensian through long residence. Although he was born in 'a little village on the Weighton river', soon afterwards he was brought to Hull. In 1815, the year of Waterloo, he had crossed the Humber to work as a gardener on the Brocklesby estate, but then it was back to Hull for the rest of his long life.

He had lived through a century of remarkable change and he could remember events from what seemed a different world. Oral history is fascinating, but all memories are fallible, and it's reassuring when personal recollections are confirmed by other sources. Thomas Leak comes well out of this test.

What particularly impressed him was the growth of Hull, whose population, he said, had increased a staggering ten times since his childhood (in fact, 24,299 in 1801 to 200,044 by 1891), and at the beginning of the century he remembered only one house on Anlaby Road between Carr Lane and the Toll Bar. Some time in 1809 or 1810 he had seen a schoolmaster fastened in the pillory 'on the ground upon which the Blind Institution stands. It was then a green field.' Presumably this was near Kingston Square: the Medical School, opened there in 1833, became the Institute for the Blind in 1870. Although Mr. Leak could not remember any public execution in Hull (the last was in 1778), he was familiar with the gruesome apparatus: 'I played upon the gallows many a score of times. They stand near Great Thornton Street and were taken down about 36 years since.'

He had also witnessed the transformation of Whitefriargate from a street with low, two-storey houses into a grander thoroughfare. He remembered the Whitefriars' Burial Ground at the corner of Trinity House Lane being done away with: 'There were bones by the score, and little pieces of old pipes which had been buried.' This would be around 1830 when Smith's Bank was built on the south side of the street. Thomas Leak was old enough to have been present at the opening of Junction Dock (later renamed Princes Dock) on 1 June 1829: 'I was in Mytongate and could even now go to the very spot where I was standing' when the Trinity House Yacht sailed in.

As for George III's Jubilee: 'The illuminations were magnificent. I have never since seen anything like them. The working population had a tea, and everyone was gay.' The King reigned 1760-1820, but never made it to the end of his 60th year on the throne, and, oddly, his Golden Jubilee was celebrated in 1809, at the start of his 50th year as a monarch, not at its completion in 1810. Centenarians were rare on the ground at that time, and Mr. Leak knew he had been lucky. When he was about 40 he suffered an illness caused by wet clothes, and eminent doctors agreed there was no hope, but after 33 weeks he recovered. He had been recommended to try gin: 'I had intended remaining a teetotaller all my life, but, finding that the gin did me good, I have continued to take a drop now and then ever since.' And he continued to defy medical opinion in another way: by daily smoking two or three pipes of 'bacca'.

BEFORE THE WAR

Hull in the 1930s

The Blitz on Hull made the years before the war seem in retrospect a vanished age when the City was taking on an increasingly smart appearance, and pleasures no longer possible had been taken for granted. Many had suffered cruelly in the Depression and its aftermath, but there were noticeable signs of recovery – and it is hardly surprising if distance lent enchantment to the view of peacetime Hull in the Thirties.

There were still slums, but the council estates were a great improvement on previous conditions and, in the biggest private building boom ever experienced in Britain, the City spread into new avenues and roads with names which have a distinctive period flavour: like Sunningdale Road (1932), Balmoral Avenue (1933) and Kenilworth Avenue (1934). This was the era of the semi-detached, a style which has stood the test of time.

One unmistakable sign of progress was the creation of improved thoroughfares to cope with the growth in traffic. North Bridge was rebuilt in 1931 and the route to it straightened, with George Street now extended to include most of Charlotte Street. Even more radical was the opening of Ferensway, which involved the demolition of much old property and the lopping-off of the end of Mill Street.

Building Societies enabled more to buy one of the new semi's, but renting was still the norm, and there were plenty of houses to let at prices ranging from 15 shillings (75p) to £1 per week. 'Within one minute of trams' was an added attraction. Trams ran until 1945, trolley buses were introduced in 1937, and train and bus services into East Yorkshire were on a scale long since diminished. In 1935 the LNER put on special trips to Hull Fair with return tickets from Driffield and Market Weighton at 1s. 6d. (7½p), Pocklington 2s. 6d. (12½p) and Broomfleet 1s. (5p).

In spite of the spread of Hull (the population in 1931 was over 300,000), it was still encircled by a wide belt of green fields,. and anyone coming into the City from outside was aware of the transition from country to town.

The No 49 bus from Hedon, for example, travelled between fields until the first industrial landmark, Salt End (only a fraction of its modern size), and then it was largely countryside again, apart from a few houses and the Cod

Ferensway.

Liver Oil factory in its rural isolation, until Marfleet (absorbed in Hull in 1882). After Marfleet the scene became distinctly urban, with docks on one side and, opposite, the crowded streets of terraced houses. On Hedon Road itself horse-drawn rullies from Rank's mill lumbered among the cars and lorries.

Wartime rationing, the later growth of self-service and supermarkets made the Thirties a Utopian age of shopping, and the names of shop are as evocative in stirring nostalgic memories as the tunes of the period. Corner shops were busy, and, like the great stores, provided personal service, with the customary chair at the counter, the individual wrapping of goods, not yet pre-packed – and home deliveries. A typical advertisement was one from Murray Bros, butchers of Hessle Road: 'Smart errand boy wanted, 14-16.'

Hull was a pioneering city for films. An earlier article mentioned the 'royal' group of cinemas opened in the Thirties, and a host of suburban cinemas flourished, often changing programme mid-week. Happy endings were preferred, and in the film version of *South Riding* true love triumphed in a way Winifred Holtby never intended.

Hull was on the itinerary of J. B. Priestley, researching his book, *English Journey,* in 1933. He had seen northern towns defeated by the Depression, 'But even the weather – and I never knew such a place for icy rain – could not make Hull look as cheerless as most big ports. It had an air of prosperity.' Soon, however, the clouds of war began to gather, and in 1935 it was reported that five Hull officials were to attend a conference on Air Raid Precautions: an ominous sign of things to come.

MARITIME MOVES
Hull's Maritime Museum

The decision to change the name of the Town Docks Museum to the Maritime Museum will revive memories of the old Maritime Museum on Hessle Road. It still stands: a pleasant, unassuming building of 1912, designed by Hull's first City Architect, the talented Joseph II. Hirst, and paid for by the philanthropic fishing magnate, Christopher Pickering. Although vastly overcrowded and with a higgledy-piggledy collection of exhibits, it was held in great affection by those who frequented it – free of charge.

There is no sign of humility in the building which, since 1975, has housed the museum in Queen Victoria Square. Proud and imposing, it holds its own in the centre of the City, a lasting symbol of Victorian confidence and of the importance of the men who commissioned it for their headquarters: the directors of the Hull Dock

Maritime Museum.

Company, who were well aware of their contribution to the prosperity of the port.

It was not Hull's first dock office. When The Dock (later Queen's Dock) opened in 1778, it had its own office, a neat Georgian building, conveniently placed on the northern side of the entrance from the River Hull, and, when Humber Dock was opened in 1809, it was also provided with its own office. Growing trade brought the need for a larger administrative block, and in 1820 the two individual buildings were replaced by a new office, opened in the northern continuation of High Street. It remains as a modest but attractive reminder of Hull's Georgian heyday.

Continuing expansion meant that only 20 years later it had to be enlarged, and, as further docks were built, it was decided to erect more spacious headquarters. The site was not the easiest which might have been chosen, a triangular area then occupied by property which had to be demolished, but it was at the very heart of the town, overlooking Monument Bridge which linked Queen's Dock and Princes Dock.

A competition for an appropriate design attracted 115 entrants, and Christopher George Wray, an architect with a substantial record both at home and abroad, emerged as the winner. Wray showed great imagination in using the odd shape of the site to create an equally unusual building, with domes at its three corners which form a distinctive feature of the Hull skyline, and the Venetian style of architecture added a touch of romance to the mundane business of the docks.

Railways enabled materials to be transported from all over England, but, amazingly, all construction was carried out by the Dock Company's employees, with specialists brought in for the rich ornamentation which makes it such a superb example of Victorian art. External sculpture represented 'Commerce, Prosperity and the River Humber', and the profusion of carved nautical items, such as fishing nets, lighthouses and seahorses, as well as tridents and harpoons on the iron railings, made it abundantly clear that this was a building with a maritime purpose.

The official opening took place on 5 October 1871 but there were more changes ahead. In 1893 the NER took over the Dock Company and henceforth both dock and railway staff were accommodated there. Less than a century after its opening, the Docks Board moved to Bond Street, and the redundant building was acquired for conversion to a museum. Yet in spite of all that has gone on within its walls, from the outside it looks as permanent and unchanging as the Victorian directors intended it to be.

SAME NAME: CHANGING SCENE

John Scott I, II and III, of St. Mary's Church, Lowgate, Hull

St. Mary's Church, Lowgate, had three 19th-century vicars, each named John Scott and each the representative of a different generation. John Scott I (Vicar 1816-34) was father of John Scott II (1834-65) and he in turn was father of John Scott III (1865-83).

It was a remarkable record, and their collective impact on the church and town was enormous, but it's a by-product of the family which probably has greater interest for local people today. John Scott II had another son, Samuel Cooper Scott, born in 1838, whose book of reminiscences, *Things That Were*, provides a fascinating insight into life in Hull and district in the early years of Victoria's reign. The first home he recalled was his birthplace in Prospect Street, now a crowded thoroughfare in the City centre, but then with lingering reminders of its rural past. The Scott's house backed on to a paddock where they would picnic in summer, and, although the grass was already dank and the trees black with soot and smoke, the birds hunting for crumbs and the smell of balsam poplars made it genuine countryside to children.

Later John Scott II and his family moved to a house in Dock Walls, near Monument Bridge. The nursery overlooked what was soon to be re-named Queen's Dock and the children spent hours enjoying their grandstand view of the colourful scene below. Their favourite was the grain ship, and they never tired of watching the unloading by men who lightened their heavy toil by singing as they worked. But a close second was the beautiful fast-sailing schooner which brought in oranges. The porter who unloaded the cargo carried a large box balanced on his flat hat, and ran like an acrobat up a series of planks until he reached the top storeys of the warehouses.

Hull was still a whaling port, a trade with a family link for the young Scotts because their maternal grandfather, Samuel Spyvee Cooper, had once owned a fleet of whalers. From their nursery window they could see whaling ships laid up for the winter in a corner of the dock. Once, on his way back from school, Samuel saw a great commotion as women with babes in arms and Trinity House boys raced to the Pier to welcome home a whaler which had been stranded in the ice and presumed lost.

A red-letter day was 1 July 1840. Even though he was so young, Samuel said he remembered being taken to a house in Belle Vue Terrace near the Humber to watch the first train leave Hull. There were crowds and decorations everywhere: 'Presently the train appeared amid intense excitement and applause. It ran rather slowly and the engine was decked with flags and garlands; it had a great copper hump on its back which glittered in the sun.'

The first station was near Dock Green, a piece of land which was a favourite playground and 'a great kite-flying place'. Soon it became the site for Railway Dock (1846); a walk to see navvies digging out the dock was another popular excursion. A lot was happening in Hull at that time and the young Scotts were often taken to see building work in progress on the new Paragon Station. When Queen Victoria arrived at the station on 13 October 1854, it was their uncle, Dr. Henry Cooper, who was mayor and who had the honour of being knighted at the end of the memorable visit.

Things That Were has some nice descriptions of the children playing around the Citadel in Drypool. One severe winter they learnt to skate on the moat and in summer they could walk on the ramparts, watch the ships on the river and, in the distance, have a view of 'the picturesque village of Paull some five miles down, celebrated for its shrimps and its shrimp teas': an idyllic picture from a world that has gone.

RECYCLING HULL'S TOWN HALL

The Victorian Town Hall

Brantingham War Memorial and Pearson Park have one surprising thing in common. Both contain part of Hull's Victorian Town Hall, demolished in the early 20th century.

Hull had been remarkably late in acquiring this building with a grandeur appropriate to its status. The earliest, much altered, Guildhall was at the southern end of the Market Place, near the opening to a narrow street known as the Butchery. So inadequate was it that the pioneering historian John Tickell, who saw it in its final days, described it in 1796 as a 'paltry mansion for so wealthy a Corporation'. This was the period when Georgian Hull was undergoing an impressive upgrading, and the Butchery was replaced by the wider Queen Street, a project which included the demolition of the old Guildhall.

Instead of using this opportunity to create something more splendid, the Corporation hesitated, and in 1805 cautiously rented Alderman Jarratt's house in Lowgate as temporary headquarters. Temporary measures have a habit of lasting a long time: the building was later purchased and, in spite of its defects, continued to be Hull's Mansion House, as it was usually called, for over half a century.

The need to have much better facilities became increasingly urgent and the decision to tackle the problem in the 1860s involved some prominent people who have been the subject of earlier articles. Zachariah Pearson, ever keen to leave his mark on Hull, proposed that a new Town Hall should be built. On the other hand, Alderman Anthony Bannister preferred improvements to the existing Mansion House. The Mayor, William Hodge, however, gave his casting vote in favour of the more ambitious scheme. The site was to be the ground occupied by the Mansion House, augmented by extra land specially purchased for the purpose. Hull Corporation was not unaware that in 1858 a magnificent Town Hall in Leeds had been opened by Queen Victoria amid scenes of great pageantry. It had been designed by Hull's most important architect, Cuthbert Brodrick, and, when he was appointed designer of a Town Hall in his native town, there was surely the hope that Hull would upstage Leeds.

Work began in earnest with the laying of the foundation stone by William Hodge on 9 October 1862, an event which today would probably attract a press photographer and a television cameraman but which Victorian Hullensians treated as a red-letter day with all the fun of a carnival, flags, a colourful procession, a civic luncheon and a mayoral banquet. The official opening on 25 January 1866 was an even grander occasion and there was justified praise for this splendid Classical building with its sumptuous interior.

Hull continued to expand and larger premises were soon required. Originally the plan was to graft an extension on to Brodrick's Town Hall. The law courts of the present Guildhall were completed in 1907, but then the controversial decision was taken to demolish the Victorian building and give architectural unity to a completely new structure. Work was completed in 1916, and Sir John Sherman, a Hull alderman who lived at Brantingham, rescued stones from the demolished building, later to be used on the village war memorial. Ironically, the cupola was placed in the park named after Pearson, whose public career had ended as prematurely as the Town Hall he so badly wanted but which lasted for barely 50 years.

Brantingham War Memorial.

84

CAPITAL OF THE WOLDS, IF NOT THE WORLD

Driffield

Driffield's likely linking with a French 'twin' should help to spread its name abroad. Rarely does it seem to receive its fair share of the spotlight, though in recent years publications by Peter Howorth (*Driffield: A Country Town in its Setting*) and David Neave (*Driffield: A Town Trail*) have focused attention on its interesting history and the high quality of its architecture.

Great Driffield – to give it the title which distinguishes it from its Little offshoot – has roots which reach back into prehistory, and in the Middle Ages its markets and fairs made it an important commercial centre. But the town which exists today is largely the product of its golden age of prosperity in late Georgian and Victorian times when three factors combined to give it a boost: the three C's: corn, Canal and communications (by road and by rail).

Improvements in agriculture in the 18th century, introduced by such landowners as Sir Christopher Sykes of nearby Sledmere, helped transform the barren Wolds into 'one of the most productive and best cultivated' areas in Yorkshire. Driffield was ideally placed as the market centre for handling vastly increased supplies of corn, and a further impetus to the growth of trade was provided in 1770 by the opening of the Canal (or, more correctly, Navigation) which gave it access by water to an expanding Hull and to the densely populated towns of the West Riding. In the 18th century transport by water was often quicker than by land, but in 1766 the journey between Beverley and Driffield was made easier by the opening of a turnpike road. There was a much more revolutionary advance in 1846 when Driffield became part of the railway network with the opening of the Hull-Bridlington line. Later lines provided links with Malton and Market Weighton.

River Head is now a tranquil, semi-rural part of Driffield, a far cry from its heyday when business on the canal boomed. The scene may have changed, but attractive buildings remain as reminders of the Georgian port area which once flourished here and warehouses have been converted into riverside residences.

Riverhead, Driffield.

Driffield was fortunate to have a number of buildings designed by distinguished architects. In the 1870s George Gilbert Scott junior restored the parish church, and Temple Moore made further alteration in the Edwardian period. Lockwood Street commemorates H.F. Lockwood, who designed a fine police station and also a Corn Exchange which became the Town Hall and is now incorporated in the Bell Hotel. This is an impressive building in its own right and has played a major role in Driffield's social, business and political life.

Lockwood's eminent pupil, Cuthbert Brodrick, built the school on Cross Hill, and William Hawe was responsible for the grandiose premises of Lance and Co and for a number of good buildings in his distinctive style. One Victorian building, the White House in Beverley Road, hides a tragic story. It was the residence of Luke White, a solicitor who served as Liberal M.P.

for Buckrose, 1900-18, but who misappropriated money from his clients' accounts, and, too ill to face trial and now a pauper, entered the Workhouse where he died. The account of his descent 'From White House to Workhouse' holds more drama than many works of fiction and deserves telling at greater length.

In the past two decades one's impression is that Driffield has succeeded in becoming smarter and more up-market without losing its character as a genuine country town, unlike those over-prettified places which live on tourism but have lost their vitality in the process. In its earlier period of prosperity Driffield was dubbed 'the Capital of the Wolds', a description which may confuse visitors from France. Foreigners often imagine that 'Wold' must be a misspelling of 'World'. Will they assume that Driffield claims to be 'the Capital of the World'?

WHEN THEY DANCED ALL NIGHT

The Assembly Rooms in Beverley and Hedon

Development plans for Beverley's dilapidated Regal cinema focus attention on the contrast between its present appearance and the balmy days when this was the ultra-smart centre of the town's social life.

Long before becoming a cinema in 1935, it had started its career as the Assembly Rooms, where the town's upper crust gathered in order to see, and be seen by, their peers. The dazzling assemblies of Bath and York had inspired smaller towns to follow suit, and so, on 11 May 1761, a group of interested gentlemen met at the Tiger in North Bar Within to discuss buying a piece of land in Norwood for £210 and financing the project by subscribing for £25 shares. John Carr, the eminent York architect, was paid ten guineas for designing an appropriately impressive building, and William Middleton, the man who did more than any

other to transform Beverley into a Georgian town, received £790 for carrying out the work. Estimates are notoriously unreliable: the expense of interior fitting and furnishing meant that a mortgage was needed to pay off the full cost.

Any presence of soldiers in the town boosted attendance at assemblies and the first function after the Rooms were ready for use in 1763 was a ball given by officers of the East Riding militia. Beverley was also a racing town, and the glitter of an evening assembly was the perfect ending to a day on the racecourse. As well as dancing, the clientèle could enjoy cards (whist was the fashionable game), drinking tea and – always popular – gossip. Correct etiquette was of supreme importance but an assembly's less formal role was providing a place where the latest news could be exchanged and romances could begin.

The opening of the Regal cinema involved the demolition of the front part of the Assembly Rooms and its replacement by a typical piece of mid-Thirties' architecture, but the large building which survives was built in 1840 to the design of H. F. Lockwood, the architect whose work in Driffield was mentioned in a recent article. In the Victorian period this hall became the venue for a whole catalogue of events. In May 1897, for example, when St. John's Catholic Church was about to be built, it was the scene of a grand fund-raising concert, arranged by Mr. Maw, interlocutor of the Beverley Minstrel and Entertainment Society, and graced by the Mayor and Mayoress: 'The Beverley Orchestral Band under the wand of Mr. Waddington gave several selections in pleasing style.'

Even Hedon, a much smaller place than Beverley, wanted to share the high life, and in the Blue Ball, an inn next to the Town Hall, affluent residents held their first assembly on 4 January 1798. It was on a far more modest scale than anything in Beverley, with the innkeeper receiving 16 shillings for the use of rooms which can hardly have had much space for dancing. Nevertheless, a strict code of behaviour was enforced: ladies were required to change partners every two dances and no gentleman was allowed to dance in boots.

As in Beverley, military men added zest to the atmosphere. Soldiers were stationed in Holderness ready to repel any invasion during the Anglo-French wars, and the Assembly held on 7 June 1798 had an injection of blue blood when visitors attending included Major General Lennox (later Duke of Richmond), Major Maxwell, five officers, Lady Charlotte Lennox and Lady Georgina Gordon.

The echoes of the music to which these privileged people danced their minuets has long since faded away. Hedon's Blue Ball was demolished in 1931 and replaced by the W.I.'s Alison Hall. At the time of writing the Regal in Beverley stands forlornly awaiting its future.★

★Work is now in progress on new developments.

NORWOOD, BEVERLEY

Former Assembly Rooms (centre); Norwood House (right).

THE WELL-TO-DO OF WELTON

Welton is one of our most attractive villages with an impressive number of fine houses in a sylvan setting. Landscape often owes as much to man as to Nature, and both appearance and architecture are the result of changes in the village in the 18th and 19th centuries.

Until that period Welton was a typical rural community with the majority of men working on farms but with a range of tradesmen which made it almost self-sufficient. A new element, though, was introduced by men who had made their money in business, particularly in Hull, and who wanted to set themselves up as country gentlemen. An old guide book describes Welton as 'shielded from chilly winds, but open to the southern sky. It is a remarkably salubrious spot and persons in a delicate state of health frequently find a short residence in the neighbourhood beneficial.'

These assets brought it a galaxy of well-to-do residents. St. Helen's Church has memorials to Robert Mason, twice Mayor of Hull, and W. Hammond, former Chairman of the Dock Company. In the early Victorian period smart villas were occupied by Rev. Thomas Galland (Welton Hill), a relative of the artist, Burne-Jones; Rev. Miles Popple (Welton Lodge), a member of an important Hull family; John Smith (Welton Garth) and John Wilkinson (Welton Grange).

But better-known than all these were the Raikes. Robert Raikes, a Hull banker, inherited

Welton House in 1814 after the death of his father-in-law, Thomas Williamson, who had rebuilt the mansion and improved its grounds and begun a transformation of the village by planting trees and shrubs, and creating pleasant walks with a rustic temple and views of the Humber. Robert Raikes continued his work, rebuilt Welton House once more, enlarged the gardens, and made further additions to the beauty of Welton, building in 1818 the Mausoleum which has become a local landmark. By preventing the Hull-Selby Railway building a station at Welton, with the result that the nearest one is at Brough, he performed a service about which modern residents may hold differing views.

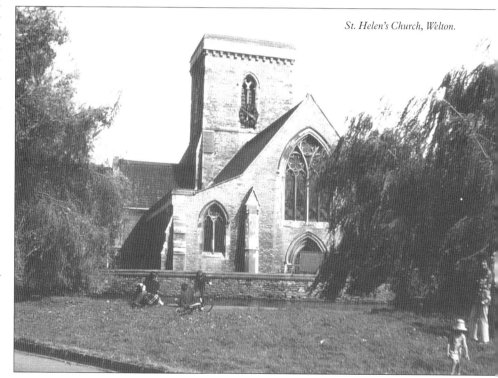

St. Helen's Church, Welton.

Much fresher in local memories than the Raikes are their successors, the Harrison-Broadleys. As the plain Broadleys they had made their fortune in trade, banking and property, and in 1849, after the death of the widowed Mrs. Raikes, Henry Broadley M.P. acquired Welton House, adding the Raikes estate to his already vast possessions. 'A man,' it was said, 'cannot pass out of Hull in any direction without walking on land at one time or at present owned by the Broadley family.' After his death in 1851 everything passed to his spinster sister, Sophia, whose main contribution to Welton was having the church restored at her own expense.

Sophia in turn left it all to her nephew, William H. Harrison (the first to double-barrel the surname), and some will recall the 'HB' sign on the gates leading to the 15,000 acres in East Yorkshire owned by him and his heir, Henry Harrison-Broadley. The Welton link was essentially lost this century when the next head of the family, Captain John, moved to Tickton Grange.

Welton House, by now too vast to be maintained, was demolished in 1952. A few items from both house and gardens were rescued and the former entrance is still clearly visible. The most important memorial to all these people of the past, however, is the ambience of Welton and the pleasant environment they created.

THE WONDERS OF WINESTEAD

Winestead is a corner of Holderness more full of history and with more links with the famous than many larger places. A description from an old directory – 'a small pleasant village surrounded by a variety of picturesque scenery' – is as true today as it was when the book was published in 1823, and there's the same timelessness in its reference to the church, 'surrounded by lofty trees that give it an air of deep solemnity'. St. Germain's, standing in seclusion away from the village, has, in fact, undergone many changes since its foundation in the 12th century though they blend in perfect harmony. It's a far more complex building than its simple exterior suggests and an excellent church for people interested in local history to visit: small enough for its evolution to be traced without being overwhelmed by the vastness of a cathedral.

Brass chandeliers and woodwork give it an atmosphere of great intimacy, almost as if it were the family chapel of the Hildyards, who have played a major part in Winestead's history. The pulpit is 17th-century, and the joiner who fitted a new door in 1694 sensibly chiselled out its date and his name. During Victorian restoration the distinguished architect, Temple Moore, moved panelling from the Georgian box pews to the walls, and other work of high quality was carried out by Beverley's own master carver, James Elwell.

Winestead has another link with an eminent architect through its lectern, designed by Sir George Gilbert Scott and given by a well-known local man, Albert Rollitt, in memory of his wife, Eleanor, who died in 1885 during their year as Mayor and Mayoress of Hull. But more famous than any of these was Andrew Marvell, baptised in the font in 1621 by his father, the Rector, and later to attain the heights as Secretary to Cromwell, M.P. for Hull, and one of the great English poets.

The 1823 directory's praise of Winestead's 'two elegant halls' has unfortunately to be amended as a result of 20th-century developments. One of these houses, Winestead Hall (often called the Red Hall), was demolished in 1936. It was replaced by a hospital, though surviving from the former mansion of the Hildyards is the stable block designed by the York architect, John Carr. The loss of the house had, however, one unintended consequence. It inspired Colonel Rupert Alec-Smith to found the Georgian Society for East Yorkshire with the aim of encouraging local people to place more value on their heritage. After the war Colonel Alec-Smith moved to the Old Rectory, where alterations were made by another renowned architect, Francis Johnson, and where he was able to incorporate examples of craftsmanship worth rescuing when the buildings containing them were demolished, among them items from Hull's High Street.

Winestead still has its White Hall, built by Arthur Maister, grandson of the man who decided to build the magnificent Maister House in Hull, after its predecessor was destroyed by fire. It's a most attractive Regency house with grand portico and neat sash and bow windows, all surrounded by the fine trees which are such a feature of the Winestead landscape. Through the Winestead story runs a chain of events with surprising consequences. When the novelist Winifred Holtby was living in Withernsea in 1934 she would see from the train the White Hall, then uninhabited and overgrown. Before starting to write her most famous book she drew a map of the fictional South Riding, placing 'Maythorpe' with its decaying hall at a point identical with Winestead. Fact and fiction met when *South Riding* was televised, and the scenes set in the imaginary 'Maythorpe Hall' were filmed at Winestead's White Hall.

SANCTON MAKES THE HEADLINES

Sancton featured in the *Hull Daily Mail* recently when Mrs. Freda Train wrote to point out that my article on King Billy made no mention of Houghton Hall, Sancton, where the statue was evacuated during the war. Mrs. Train is deeply loyal to Sancton, where she spent her childhood, and, once I had contacted her to explain that the reference to Houghton Hall in my original article had been excluded for reasons of space at the editorial stage, our little local difficulty was quickly resolved and I was invited to visit her and her husband, Edwin, in Brantingham.

They know the whole area extremely well because work has taken them to so many different places. King Billy, Mrs. Train remembers, spent the war standing on grass at the rear of Houghton Hall, clearly visible to passers-by. Her mother, Mrs. Hatfield, worked at the Hall for years and Mrs. Train was there briefly at the beginning of the war. The size and grandeur of the mansion made a strong impression on her and she recalls the days when Sancton children had to curtsey to Colonel Langdale's wife if they wanted to be on her list for a present of sweets at Christmas.

As I had mentioned earlier, it was an irony of history that this Catholic family should give refuge to the statue of William III, especially as their ancestor, Lord Langdale, the Governor of Hull's Citadel, had been overpowered in a Protestant rising in 1688, soon after the accession of the King. With information from Mrs. Train I was able to find the Catholic cemetery at Sancton where the Langdales are buried and where they have a tiny memorial chapel, though the main chapel at the Hall was demolished in 1959.

Mr. Edwin Train's career as a gardener made him familiar with a number of large homes in the area, and his recollections give history an immediacy which books often fail to convey. Both before and after the war he was at Welton House. It was then unoccupied, though some youths in the know got access to the cellars where bottles of sherry lingered. He was working for a member of another well-known family, Mr. John Bladon, at Wolfreton Garth, Kirkella, when

Welton House was demolished in 1952, and he is amazed that so many great houses were allowed to disappear in those post-war years before legislation was introduced to control such destruction.

Brantinghamthorpe was the house with which he had the longest connection. Even before he started work there in 1959 his father was a gardener for Sir John Sherman, the Hull doctor and civic leader, who moved to Brantinghamthorpe in 1909. In his father's time the gardens were maintained in all their glory, just as they had been created by James Craig Niven, Hull's talented park and garden designer, for Christopher Sykes M.P. who wanted grounds of suitable magnificence where the Prince of Wales (later Edward VII) and other royal and noble guests could stroll. Mr. Train senior had been one of eight gardeners but, by the time his son went to Brantinghamthorpe, the world had changed and the only person Edwin had to help him was his father. Edwin Train's spontaneous praise of Mr. and Mrs. Maxsted, who then lived there, makes it clear that he enjoyed the happiest working relationship with his employers, for whom he retains the highest regard.

Local people tend to be too parochial in their knowledge of our area, and for someone like myself whose roots are to the east of the City it was all a pleasant reminder of the wealth of interest which lies at t'other side of Hull.

A TALE OF TWO CHURCHES

The Minster and St. Mary's Church, Beverley

The Minster and St. Mary's are such an integral part of Beverley that it takes a leap of imagination to see them as separate structures detached from the surrounding clutter of everyday life. This is where the exhibition at Beverley's Art Gallery, 'A Tale of Two Churches', comes in useful. Many of the pictures on display focus on these buildings rising from the ground in magnificent isolation, revealing how much is lost or taken for granted even by people who claim to know them well.

It's a reminder too that, though buildings need firm foundations, they rarely remain the same for long, but adapt to cope with changing needs and ideas. Beverley Minster, for example, experienced a series of radical alterations in the 18th century which today would cause an outcry from planning committees and conservation groups. At that time it was in a shameful state of disrepair and there was a desperate need to do something about the north transept gable, which was leaning dangerously outwards. William Thornton, a York carpenter, designed a massive timber framework which in 1719-20 enabled the wall to be screwed back into upright, and the distinguished architect, Nicholas Hawksmoor, supervised a restoration programme which included installing an ornate altar-piece, choir screen and nave galleries and – something not easily avoidable – an onion-shaped cupola fixed on the stub tower. It was not to everyone's taste, and, when Mary Wordsworth travelled through Beverley in 1802, she described the Minster as ' a pretty clean building but injured very much with Grecian architecture'. Sufficient Beverlonians agreed with her for the dome and other classical 'improvements' to be removed 1824-7.

Some of the pictures in this excellent exhibition are well-known, but it is an opportunity to see works from the Art Gallery Collection not normally on display. Two early 19th-century paintings by J.C. Buckler are most attractive and atmospheric period pieces, and his views of the Minster are tinged with gentleness and quiet beauty.

Beverley's growth in a northerly direction created the need for St. Mary's, originally a more convenient chapel of ease of the Minster but by the 16th century a parish church in its own right. Its architectural development is more complex than the Minster's and made even more complicated by the fall of the tower in 1520 and its replacement by the present one, of such perfect proportions that this disaster can, at least in retrospect, be regarded as a happy accident.

St. Mary's has never ceased to attract artists and photographers, and another painting in this exhibition by Buckler showing St. Mary's in 1804 is as delightful as those of the Minster and with the bonus of an intriguing glimpse of Hengate in the background. Thomas B. Burton's work is at last receiving the recognition it deserves, and Caroline A. Brereton's pictures are always conceived with great delicacy. There's a pleasant touch of intimacy in her paintings of a group at the font in 1852 and of the occupants of the Corporation pew.

The Minster and St. Mary's were, after all, not created merely to be examples of great architecture. They were built to be used by people, and it's important to remember their human aspects. A religious census conducted on 30 March 1851 shows an attendance at the Minster of 386 adults and 213 children in the morning, with 492 adults and 236 children present on the afternoon. Seats were in such demand that the Minster had an offshoot, St. John's in Lairgate, opened in 1840. On census Sunday it had congregations of approximately 400 at both morning and evening services. Declining congregations caused its closure in 1939, and after the war it was converted into the Memorial Hall.

THE EAST COMES TO EAST YORKSHIRE

Kilnwick Percy Hall

An East Yorkshire stately home and Eastern philosophy seem worlds apart – but they come together at Kilnwick Percy Hall near Pocklington, now the nationally important Madhyamaka Buddhist Centre. It stands in a beautiful setting at the foot of the Wolds and, well before you arrive, you look across the wooded landscape and catch a view of the great house. All is so peaceful that it's easy to understand why people of all beliefs come here to relax and free themselves from the stresses of modern living.

Built in the early 18th century, Kilnwick Percy Hall went through a number of transformations before achieving its present appearance. Originally the home of the Anderson family, it was substantially altered by a new owner, Robert Denison, an influential figure in local Tory politics in the early 19th century.

But it was his successor, Admiral the Hon. Arthur Duncombe, purchaser of the estate in 1840, who gave the house the grandeur which remains its most lasting feature. The Duncombes were a typical example of a family whose members were upwardly mobile and, after making their money in business, bought land, married into the aristocracy, entered Parliament and acquired a title. The Admiral was a younger son of Lord Feversham of Duncombe Park, Helmsley, and before settling at Kilnwick Percy he had married an heiress and become M.P. for Retford.

His impact on the Hall was considerable. To its exterior he added a parapet and – even more prominent – the massive portico. Internally the emphasis was on ostentation, with a grand staircase, imitation marble columns, decorative plaster-work, and, grandest of all, a ballroom with rich panelling. To complement this splendour there were pleasure gardens, spacious lawns, acres of parkland and a lake. Admiral Duncombe's estate of more than 4,000 acres brought him an income of over

Kilnwick Percy Hall,

£7,000 p.a., and wealth automatically made him one of the county's grandees, a High Sheriff, Deputy Lieutenant, and an M.P. for the East Riding 1851-68.

Kilnwick Percy itself is a deserted village but the superb little church, St. Helen's, remains just a stone's-throw from the Hall. It's Norman in origin, and a beautifully restored doorway leads to a much more sophisticated interior than one would expect in such a rural church. Wealthy people of the past completed their education by making the Grand Tour, and there is a remarkable collection of woodwork which Robert Denison brought back from the Continent.

'Upstairs, Downstairs' was a TV programme which stimulated the interest in that other world of the country house: the activities of the army of servants who sustained the lifestyle of the privileged who inhabited the fine rooms beyond the green baize door. Roger Mason's book, *Plain Tales from Yorkshire*, contains an account of Jenny Porter, a Beverley keelman's daughter, who in 1907 went to work at St. Mary's Manor for Admiral Duncombe's younger son, George Augustus, a banker. He spent much of his time at Kilnwick Percy Hall, which had been inherited by his elder brother, and reluctantly Jenny obeyed orders to move there as a scullery maid. A dangerous member of the family kept upstairs under close supervision makes her story read like something out of *Jane Eyre*.

No melodrama now disturbs the tranquil atmosphere of Kilnwick Percy Hall, and the thousands of inquiries received after the Centre was featured in a BBC holidays programme showed how many are desperately seeking such an oasis of calm.

LOCAL BOY MAKES GOOD
Charles Henry Wilson, Lord Nunburnholme

When St. James, Warter, now a redundant church, was opened during a recent heritage weekend it gave local people the opportunity of a guided tour of a building famous not only for the high quality of its stained glass and sculpture but also for its links with Hull's greatest shipping family, the Wilsons.

Everyone has heard of Arthur Wilson of Tranby Croft and the Baccarat Case but the focus of attention at Warter is his brother, Charles Henry, who rarely receives his fair share of the limelight. He was a more important figure in the family firm and in public life than Arthur and he is the Wilson commemorated in Hull by an imposing statue at the junction of Alfred Gelder Street and Lowgate.

His particular achievement was to be the first in the family to be elected to Parliament, serving over 30 years, as a Hull M.P. The Wilsons had contributed so

Lord Nunburnholme

94

much to the prosperity of the port that many shared the belief that 'What was right for the Wilsons was right for Hull', and, although he was a Liberal, he attracted much support from electors who would otherwise have been Tory.

Wealth enabled the family to marry into the aristocracy, and in 1871 Charles married Florence Wellesley, the niece of the Duke of Wellington. They made their home at what is now Hull University's Thwaite Hall, but an M.P. with a wife from the upper échelons of society needed a London residence and nothing could have been smarter than their address: 41 Grosvenor Square, Belgravia. In addition there was a villa in Nice and, later, The Bungalow, Cottingham, now Cleminson Hall.

A gentleman also needed a country estate. In 1878 Wilson bought Warter Priory, and over the following years transformed the mansion into the stateliest of homes. The envious sneered at the Wilsons for being 'rich but vulgar', yet all the evidence is that they were people of considerable taste who commissioned the best architects and craftsman for their projects and the most talented artists for their portraits.

There were royal guests at Warter as well as Tranby: in 1887 Prince Albert Victor, Duke of Clarence, arrived at Pocklington station to be greeted by hearty cheers and the ringing of the church bells. Unlike her husband, Mrs. Wilson was a Tory and allowed the home to be used for Tory functions. She was very aware that hers was the more distinguished ancestry and she was heard to boast that, although he had the money, she had 'the blood'.

In 1906, however, Charles crowned the Wilson's achievements with a peerage and took the title Lord Nunburnholme. He died the following year but Lady Nunburnholme lived on until 1932 and is still remembered as an imperious chatelaine who terrified tenants. St. James Church contains fine marble monuments by Sir George Frampton R.A., one to Lord and Lady Nunburnholme, and one to their daughter-in-law, Lady Isabel, who died at the age of 26.

Beyond the church are the graves of Lord Nunburnholme and members of his family, originally in the grounds of Warter Priory but moved after the house was sold to the Vesteys in 1929, a sad resting place for a man of such distinction. Warter Priory itself was demolished in 1972, but Lord Nunburnholme's statue stands as proudly as ever in Hull, not far from the old Town Hall, the scene of his many election victories.

SEPTEMBER SUNDAY IN HOTHAM

East Yorkshire looked at its best on a perfect autumn afternoon. There were no mists to obscure the view of a peaceful countryside warmed by the September sun, but plenty of mellow fruitfulness and rich yellows and reds in gardens along the way. Hotham is a text-book example of an English village with its long Main Street bordered by old farmhouses and cottages, a pub and a picturesque church, and the idyllic scene was complete with the sun shining brightly on St. Oswald's Church as it held its flower festival.

St. Oswald's distinctive feature is its no-nonsense Norman tower, looking as permanent and immovable as if it had grown there naturally like the trees nearby. Inside, there's the feeling of intimacy and humanity a building acquires when it's always been at the heart of a community. The font has been there since the 18th century and the Royal Arms on display are those of George III, but later generations have also left their mark. Both the Victorians and Edwardians undertook restoration, and some colourful stained glass was installed from the 1930s onwards. Things have a habit of turning up miles from their original home, and the church has much older glass, salvaged from York Minster after a disastrous 19th-century fire.

Probably most fascinating to modern visitors is the

squire's pew, reached by a private staircase, with its own fireplace and balcony view of the proceedings below so that a supervisory eye could be maintained over tenants and servants by the Lord of the Manor. In the last century this was Colonel E. J. Stracey Clitherow of Hotham Hall. By one of those odd quirks of history, the Hotham family, who take their name from the village where they were originally based, now live in South Dalton.

A 19th-century directory dismisses St. Oswald's as having 'no monuments of sufficient interest to demand notice': a strange comment on a church which has a memorial carved by George Earle junior, a member of the distinguished Hull family of sculptors, and another splendid one to the Rev. James Stillingfleet, rector for nearly 56 years, 1771-1826. No doubt the thought of leaving such a pleasant spot made it easier to turn his back on tempting offers from elsewhere. His neatly worded memorial describes him as a gentleman and a scholar who was so 'unambitious of worldly distinction' that he was content to spend his long life in such a 'retired parish'. Soon after arriving in Hotham he built what is now The Old Rectory, a most attractive house from that period when domestic architecture was at its peak, and with a garden which provided a most agreeable setting for visitors taking afternoon tea during the festival weekend.

A century ago Hotham was a far more self-contained village. Mrs. Ann Pinchon kept a virtual multiple store as grocer, draper and postmistress, Mrs. Elizabeth Pearson operated a business as joiner and wheelwright, and another one in this formidable array of emancipated women was Mrs. Elizabeth Withill, watchmaker and gun repairer. Hotham also had a tailor and blacksmith, and for those whose needs could not be satisfied locally there was Thomas Moverley, who not only dealt in potatoes but on Tuesdays and Fridays travelled with his carrier's cart to the Bull and Sun in Mytongate, Hull.

Villages need constant, though subtle, renewal if they are to retain their vitality, and it's reassuring to see in Hotham a fine new house designed by the firm of Francis Johnson of Bridlington, the architect who insisted on bringing the finest traditions of the past into the modern world.

St. Oswald's Church, Hotham.

FRIENDLY RIVALS: HEDON AND HULL

Hedon has such a long, proud history of independence that it's easy to understand concern that a large housing development on its western approaches will encroach still further on the green belt separating it from Hull. A desire to maintain its identity and individual character should not be interpreted as hostility to the City, though in the past Hedon people felt intense resentment at what they regarded as their upstart neighbour.

Trade was at the heart of the hostility. In the 12th century Hedon had been established as a port with considerable natural advantages. It was only a mile south of Preston, on which the roads of the area converged, and it was on a waterway, the Haven, which led via the Humber to the North Sea and so gave access to the Continent. The port prospered, and the wealth of its merchants enabled three churches to be built: St. James and St. Nicholas, as well as the one which survives, St. Augustine's.

This rapid rise was, unfortunately, fated to be short-lived. Hedon was too far inland to be a port with great potential. Larger ships could not use the narrow Haven, which, in any event, tended to silt, and the rise of two rival ports, Ravenser Odd and Hull (which had originated in the hamlets of Wyke and Myton) seriously damaged its trade. Although Ravenser Odd's precarious position brought its commerce to a more abrupt end than ever Hedon was to experience and by the mid-

14th century was under the sea, Hull had a golden future in store. In 1293 it received the benefit of royal patronage when it was taken over by Edward I, and in 1299 it was granted its first charter.

When Hedon acquired its own charter in 1348, the great days were already in the past, yet the benefactors of St. Augustine's kept faith with their ambitious plan and completed the church with a tower. The other two churches fell into disuse and ultimately into oblivion. The Tudor

Hedon Haven: the remains of the waterway which brought wealth to the town.

chronicler, John Leland, who visited Hedon around 1540, saw a sad picture of once-thriving docks overgrown with reeds. 'Truth is,' he wrote, 'that when Hull began to flourish Hedon decayed.'

No wonder that James Iveson, the haughty Town Clerk of Hedon, made no attempt to conceal his low opinion of Hull when he commented in 1821, 'It is a place I don't like, nor the people who live there.' At that time the distance between Hedon and Hull was greater. There was no direct Hedon Road, and the route was along Holderness Road and through Bilton and Preston. Coaches provided public transport between Patrington and Hull on five days of the week, and in 1814 Joseph Wing proudly announced that he had acquired an excellent new coach with fares of 2s. (10p) inside, and 1s. 6d. (7½p) outside.

It was obvious that a road alongside the Humber would save considerable time, and in 1830 discussions began with a view to petitioning Parliament to grant permission for a new turnpike road between Hedon and Hull. Holders of land over which the road would pass had to be satisfied, and there were traders in Hedon who complained that travellers would now bypass the main street where most of the inns and shops were situated. In spite of all the difficulties – and a financial shortfall while the project was in progress – Hedon Road was at last opened on some unidentifiable date 1832-3. The distance was shortened, but Hedon and Hull remain separate communities. In 1999 Hedon people do not begrudge Hull's celebration of the 700th anniversary of the granting of its charter.

HULL'S UNLUCKY ARCHITECT

Cuthbert Brodrick

Cuthbert Brodrick, the distinguished 19th-century architect, would be surprised and puzzled to learn that one of his buildings is to become something called Pizza Express.

The building in question, Nos. 37-9 North Bar Within, Beverley, formerly the Yorkshire Water Authority premises, began life as a pair of semi-detached houses. An advertisement in the local press on 27 July 1861 invited builders to submit tenders to the Charitable Trustees of Beverley, who had Brodrick's

Cuthbert Brodrick from Derek Linstrum's Towers and Colonnades *(Leeds 1999).*

plans and specifications available for inspection. Though Pevsner's Guide considers the red-brick Victorian block 'out of place in this predominantly Georgian street', it is in itself a sensible, unostentatious building (now Listed Grade II), and an assurance has been given that the new usage will not harm its appearance.

Brodrick has already been mentioned a number of times in this series, in articles on Hull's Victorian Town Hall, on Driffield (the Cross Hill School), and on Withernsea (Railway Station and Queen's Hotel), and his name crops up all over the East Riding with his credits making up a list of such variety that it includes Paull Vicarage, Yokefleet Hall, and restoration work at All Saints, Hessle, and St. Mary's, Beverley.

His career is all the more fascinating for holding a mystery. He was born in 1822 into a middle-class Hull family involved in shipping, and, after completing articles to H. F. Lockwood (who did so much work at Driffield), he travelled on the Continent and developed a knowledge and love of Classical architecture which was to surface in his own designs. Brodrick enjoyed early success in Hull, though the 20th century has not been kind to his buildings in his native town. His Town Hall was demolished, his lodges and chapels in the Spring Bank Cemetery have gone, and his first important building in Hull, the Royal Institution in Albion Street, was destroyed in the blitz on 24 June 1943.

It was commissioned by two influential organisations, the Hull Literary and Philosophical Society and the Subscription Library, which wanted headquarters of a grandeur fitting their importance, and Brodrick's design resulted in a building described as 'one of the chief ornaments of the town'. The laying of the foundation stone on 17 May 1853 was blessed with a cloudless sky and glorious sunshine, and thousands lined the streets to see a colourful procession make its way from the Public Rooms (now the New Theatre) to the site. But even more important was the day it received its royal accolade. When Queen Victoria visited Hull in 1854, Prince Albert made an early-morning visit on 14 October to inspect the newly-completed building with its Corinthian-columned entrance ('like the Louvre at Paris') and its magnificent interior. Eventually it became the Municipal Museum and at the time of its destruction was giving refuge to the already bombed-out Thornton-Varley's.

By the time he built the North Bar Within houses Brodrick had moved to Leeds, which has been luckier than Hull with the survival of some of his finest buildings, the Town Hall and Corn Exchange. In Scarborough too his Grand Hotel stands as proudly as ever. He had begun so brilliantly that mystery surrounds his decision to give up architecture when he was only 47. Though he did not die until 1905, his career was over. A taste for the Gothic had replaced the Classical style he preferred, and probably disappointment at the rejection of his plans accounts to some extent for his early retirement – and tragic waste of talent. Pizza Express sounds incongruous, but at least it gives a Brodrick building a new lease of life.

MAIL – AND FEMALE
Hull's General Post Office

Hull's former General Post Office stands with such grandeur at the junction of Lowgate and Alfred Gelder Street that its proposed conversion into a hi-tech centre* may seem a come-down for one of the City's finest buildings in the 'Edwardian Imperial' style. Yet its future is in keeping with its past. When it was opened in 1909 great emphasis was placed on the up-to-the-minute equipment which would enable it to deal more efficiently with the vastly increased quantities of mail created by the growth of the port. There had been earlier post offices – in Bishop Lane, Land of Green Ginger, Whitefriargate, and, from 1877, in the

*The building has become a public house and apartments.

Market Place – but even that grand four-storied building was superseded by the new GPO with 'its stately proportions and its noble design and decoration', and its 'handsome and spacious hall'.

When the Post Master General, the Rt. Hon. Sydney Buxton M.P., arrived by train to perform the opening ceremony on 22 July 1909 he was not greeted by the large crowd which usually assembled in that period to welcome a Cabinet Minister. The time had been kept secret to foil an expected suffragette demonstration – a wise precaution as the PMG was soon to discover. Miss Marsh, organiser of the Women's Social and Political Union in Leeds, was aware of the rest of the day's programme and was determined to approach the distinguished guest when he toured Riverside Quay. The police restrained her, she struggled to get free, and in 'jerky sentences' protested that this was a public place where she had every right to be. 'Never mind your rights,' she was told. 'You are not going to get near Mr. Buxton.' 'I don't want to get near him. I only want votes for women,' she explained. But the officer was disinclined to get into a political argument and dismissed her plea with the reprimand used to quell naughty children: 'Now, don't be silly.' Such a fearless woman was equally disinclined to accept defeat and, when she was released, promised the police 'they would see her later in the day'.

True to her word, as Buxton approached the door of the new building at the official opening, Miss Marsh ('wearing a long, light mackintosh in which the flushed female swayed to and fro') moved forward to a mixed reception of applause and sarcasm from the crowd. This time she was hurried off to the Central Police Station, where she settled down cheerfully to read a newspaper, obviously bearing no grudge against the police for doing their duty.

The site of the GPO has its own fascinating history. It was one of the earliest occupied parts of the medieval town when Edward I's royal official, the bailiff, established his residence there in 1297. Later, and more famously, it became the Manor House of the De la

Poles, and was known as the Suffolk Palace after they acquired their hereditary title: a substantial building of over 20 rooms with hall, tower and chapel in nine-acre gardens. It was there that Henry VIII stayed in 1541. By that time it had become the King's Manor and the weaponry stored there was Charles I's objective in trying – unsuccessfully – to gain entrance to Hull in 1642.

Thereafter it was downhill all the way with demolition and disrepair. Fairs were held in the grounds in the 17th century, and at different times in the next century Baptists, then Methodists used the tower as a meeting house. A prosperous merchant, Robert Broadley, bought the property for later building streets and, though some were lost when Alfred Gelder Street was built, Manor Street remains as a survival of this development and of the great house. With such a chequered past it's unlikely that the new development will be the last chapter in the story.

Plaque on the site of the Suffolk Palace.

A VICTORIAN DIARY DISCOVERED

The diary of a 19th-century Winestead gardener

Winestead is very dear to the heart of Mr. Ken Fussey, and, after reading my recent article on the village, he phoned to tell me how much the place means to him and his conviction that many pages of its history are still to be written. In his words: 'There's more to Winestead than Andrew Marvell.'

The phone call led to a visit to his home – in Patrington – though all his working life has been spent in Winestead since his first job at Red Hall Farm when he was 16. The Red Hall itself had been demolished in 1936 (though he points out that the walled garden is still there) and his long experience as a gardener, under a succession of employers, has given him an intimate knowledge of its grounds.

The highlight of my visit was seeing a copy of a diary written in Winestead over 130 years ago which has found its way back there by a remarkable route. When Lincolnshire-born gardener, Samuel Todd, then 24, moved from Lord Yarburgh's estate at Brocklesby to take up a post at Winestead House on 28 April 1858, he began his diary the day he started, and kept it conscientiously until he left in 1862 to emigrate to South Africa. It was his grand-daughter, on holiday in England, who found Mr. Fussey, and with

great excitement visited Winestead and left a copy of the diary which she had transcribed and edited.

Mr. Fussey thinks it disappointing that Samuel Todd included relatively few names or references to local events. Yet it conveys the authentic flavour of the routine of a large country house in the early part of Victoria's reign. In its very ordinariness, too, it reflects the steady rhythm of a gardener's life, season by season, when everything depended on the weather (recorded unfailingly each day), and manual tasks were carried out uncomplainingly by a young man who took quiet pride in his knowledge and skill.

White Hall, Winestead.

Landmarks were the days when the first cucumber was cut and the first dish of asparagus was ready, and Samuel dutifully listed the evocative names of the fruits and vegetables in his care, among them Flour Ball Potatoes, Tennis Ball Lettuce and Hessle Pears. There were all the flowers you would expect to find in an English country garden: lily of the valley, violets and tea roses ('planting sweet briar roses' was an entry in March 1861), as well as geranium, heliotropes, delphinium and rhododendrons.

His employers at Winestead House were Captain and Mrs. C.W. Goad, probably tenants of the Hildyard's, who were then having serious money problems, and great attention was paid to the fruits cultivated for the family's dessert: nectarines, peaches and apricots. The diary records the Goad's visits to London, Brantingham and Rowley as well as the arrival of guests at Winestead and there is a faint echo of the film, *The Remains of the Day*, as, at a distance Samuel watches their coming and goings while he weeds the carriage drive and mows the lawn in front of the dining room windows.

Though so discreet, he could not help disclosing the thrill of those golden days when he saw the love of his life, his Darling Annie, whose identity he always concealed from prying eyes with the initials, D.A. As he wrote on 29 July 1859: 'Fine day. Wind N.E. Hoeing and weeding and spent the day at Hull with my D.A.'

The Hildyard's sold the property in 1862, and this must have been the reason 'Mr. Goad gave me kindly notice about leaving.' In April that year he married 'D.A.', Sarah Ann Bishop, and on 26 June 1862 they sailed for Port Natal. Samuel Todd was no Samuel Pepys but he left behind a fascinating piece of local history.

FOCUS ON KING BILLY – RARE PHOTOGRAPHS FROM A READER
The statue of William III

King Billy's statue has become the 'King Charles' Head' of this column – impossible to keep out of the story for long. It all began with an article about the background to Hull's enthusiasm for honouring William III with a suitable piece of heroic sculpture, and this led to a meeting with Mrs. Freda Train to hear her memories of the statue during its wartime evacuation to Houghton Hall, Sancton.

I mentioned then how fascinating it would be to see a photograph of King Billy in his rural retreat, and now a reader of the *Hull Daily Mail*, Mr. Ron Mawer, has granted my wish. More fully, in fact, than I ever expected because he has kindly lent me two photographs. They belong to the company for which he works, Norman Walker (Machinery) Ltd, who brought King Billy back to Hull after the war. I am grateful to their Managing Director, Mr. Simon Biggs, for permission to reproduce these rare pictures. Both are of great historical interest, but particularly so is the one with Houghton Hall in the background.

King Billy was not evacuated until the fourth year of the war, in April, 1943, but it was a wise precaution in view of the raids still to come. The City Engineer's Department was responsible for organising the removal and discovered that the statue weighed just over five tons (not the seven anticipated) and that 'the feet of the charger were simply set into the stone base, the statue not being secured by any other means'.

Seeing such a long-established resident of the Old Town leave Hull naturally stirred many memories. Mr. William Jackson, who had served many years as a smith in the City Engineer's Department, recalled being given the task of improving the support under one hoof. In a different vein, another elderly man looked back to his childhood (probably in the 1870s) when Methodist meetings were held at the statue at 8 am on Sunday mornings. So great was the crowd that four ministers addressed the congregation simultaneously but from different corners of the base.

King Billy returned to Hull only in 1948, the principal reason for the delay being finance. The cost, £250, seems extremely modest by today's standards, but there was much to do in the City in those years and the Council believed that other work deserved priority. Mr. William Broady, a Hull-born industrialist, then 74, who had great affection for the statue and longed to see it back in its familiar spot, came to the rescue and generously paid the full cost himself. Scaffolding was erected, and Mr. Norman Walker, responsible for the return journey, explained that the 'heavy statue will travel on a low-loading machinery transporter'. Hence the photographs of this historic event.

King Billy was back in Hull over a year before the official unveiling on 10 October 1949. The Lord Mayor and Sheriff led a procession from the Guildhall, and Mr. Broady duly made a speech and pulled a blue cloth to reveal the newly gilded statue. One guest at the ceremony was the distinguished local historian, Mr. Ken MacMahon, who delighted his adult education classes with his account of that memorable day. There were, he said, suppressed smiles when Mr. Broady spoke poetically of 'being born under this statue' – he was referring to his home in nearby Mytongate, not to the subterranean toilets – and, during the proceedings, a dray horse which had drawn up behind the dignitaries began munching the fur on the hood of a gowned professor from the University College. Oral history of this kind helps to add a little colour to the official accounts.

King Billy on the move.

UNHOLY EVENTS AT HOLY TRINITY

Holy Trinity Church, Hull, will be the venue for another memorable event in its long history when it provides the venue for the forthcoming concert by Sir Cliff Richard. Yet, however unusual the occasion, Holy Trinity will be able to take it in its stride – in its time it has witnessed some very odd happenings. Although the church is now a haven of tranquillity offering welcome relief from the bustle of the world outside, there have been times when conditions inside were equally noisy.

One reason is that in the past there were far fewer public buildings available for everyday use, and our ancestors often treated a church with less respect than would now be acceptable. From the Reformation until the mid-17th century, Hull Corporation sometimes held its meetings in the church, and the atmosphere in the Council Room, a former chantry chapel, would be anything but sacred. When the Corporation acquired its first fire engine in 1673, Holy Trinity was the convenient central location for this new vehicle. In 1743 the first rudimentary fire brigade was formed, and regular practices as well as real emergencies created another disturbance of the peace.

But nothing equalled the disruption caused by the clergy themselves in the years following the Civil War, when religion and politics had become so closely intertwined and sectarian cliques were appallingly intolerant of each other's beliefs. William Styles, appointed Vicar in 1642, did not enjoy an easy relationship with the church's argumentative Presbyterian lecturer (preacher), John Shawe, and the Corporation had to settle their dispute about which of them should preach on Sunday mornings.

The unholy state of affairs reached its climax in the 1650s when religious rivalry put into opposing camps the civilian residents and the staunchly Puritan military in the garrison. To accommodate their differing viewpoints a wall was built inside the church, across the chancel and transepts, so that John Shawe could conduct his services in the nave while John Canne, the Governor's chaplain, could preach to the soldiers at the east end. The noise level rose as the wall did not reach the ceiling and the two congregations held simultaneous services. To reach their section, Mr. Canne's followers had to make an undignified entry via a window of the de la Pole chapel and then through the arch above the tomb into the chancel aisle.

A meeting to elect churchwardens sounds an innocuous occasion, but the feeling in Holy Trinity was anything but amicable on 22 April 1832 when one of the three candidates for the post of People's Warden was James Acland, a Radical agitator, who had arrived in Hull the previous year and begun a campaign against the undemocratic Corporation which was so inflammatory that it took the town to the edge of revolution. His reason for intervening at Holy Trinity was the parish rate which, he claimed, would produce more than the £100 needed to be raised towards the Vicar's salary. The two other candidates spoke briefly, but Acland, a man who always gave an audience full value, made a two-hour speech which was rewarded with great applause, and later, with a massive vote which made him an easy winner.

His period in office was interrupted by a spell in prison, and when he left Hull in 1835 he took with him £27 of church funds. After such turbulent events, Holy Trinity will find a Cliff Richard concert no problem.

LOOK BACK WITH JOY

Hull's Little Theatre

Hull's Little Theatre – the forerunner of the New Theatre – is another local name which revives happy memories. It began life as the Hull Repertory Theatre in 1924, and the Little Theatre Company was formed in 1928 to acquire the premises used for their performances in Kingston Square, a former lecture hall adjacent to the Assembly Rooms (now the New Theatre).

No one has more vivid and pleasant memories of those days than Mrs. Edith Waddingham who, as Edith Lister, lived not far away in Egginton Street and whose best friend, Joyce Mason, now Mrs. Tong, lived even nearer in John Street. Both girls were fascinated by the glamour of the stage and the people associated with it. Sometimes actors rehearsed in 'the Oval', the private garden in Kingston Square with access only to key holders, and by some means – Mrs. Waddingham thinks Joyce's grandfather may have paid an annual fee to Madame Clapham, the formidable dressmaker, – the two girls were able to enter the garden and picnic beneath the trees.

But the greatest thrill was to be so near to the actors, watch their rehearsals, and, on rare occasions, even speak to one of those beings from another world. There was certainly no lack of talent at the Little Theatre in the 30s and a number who gained their early experience in Hull became international stars. The roll of honour includes James Mason, Maurice Denham, William Mervyn and James Stewart Granger, who later dropped the 'James' to avoid confusion with his American counterpart.

Mrs. Waddingham's father was in the fire brigade, then part of the police force, and had to live in easy distance of the Worship Street station. It was by no means a wealthy area but, like many people who were young in the 20s and 30s, Mrs. Waddingham is convinced that, in spite of terrible poverty, public behaviour was far better than it is today. The streets were safer and there was plenty of free entertainment. On Monday evenings all seats at the Little Theatre were 1s 6d (7½p). Those who wanted to be certain of an orchestra stall would pay Edith a few pence to keep a place for them

The Little Theatre occupied the site to the left of the New Theatre.

105

at the head of the queue and she would sit on the theatre steps and watch the world go by. Quite often there were buskers, street organs and 'Stop Me and Buy One' ice-cream sellers. At other times she enjoyed the sound of music coming from the Christ Church School, then a dance hall named The Magic Lantern, and there was the outdoor drama of the processions from St. Charles Catholic Church which always thrilled her.

Her opportunity to join the staff of the Little Theatre came when she left school. At lunchtimes she worked at the Pacific Club in High Street but in the evenings she was a chocolate seller in the theatre. It was a centre of social life, the audience wore evening dress, many had their regular seats and, as she says, bought the same brand of chocolate each week. The atmosphere was as sophisticated as in any West End theatre and Edith admired the courtesy of the patrons, the diction of the actors, and the agreeable manner of Peppino Santangelo, appointed general manager in 1933.

Old programmes reveal a remarkable series of classic plays, among them *Hobson's Choice, George and Margaret* and *Escape Me Never.* They were comfortable plays. There was no *Look Back in Anger* – and Mrs. Waddingham herself looks back with great joy.